Asian Tapas And Wild Sushi

Asian Tapas and Wild Sushi

A Nibbler's Delight of Fusion Cooking

TREVOR HOOPER

Kodansha International
New York • Tokyo • London

Kodansha America, Inc.
114 Fifth Avenue, New York, New York 10011, U.S.A.

Kodansha International Ltd.
17-14 Otowa 1-chome, Bunkyo-ku, Tokyo 112, Japan

Published in 1998 by Kodansha America, Inc.
by arrangement with Whitecap Books, Vancouver/Toronto.

Library of Congress Cataloging-in-Publication Data
Hooper, Trevor.
    Asian tapas and wild sushi : a nibbler's delight of fusion cooking /
  Trevor Hooper.
       p.   cm.
     Includes index.
     ISBN 1-56836-215-3 (pbk.)
     1. Appetizers.   2. Cookery, Oriental.   3. Sushi.   I. Title.
  TX740.H618   1998
  641.8'12—dc21   97-38623

Manufactured in Canada

98 99 00 01 02   10 9 8 7 6 5 4 3 2 1

To my grandmother, Molly Hooper,

who always wanted another writer

in the family.

Acknowledgments

I would like to acknowledge and thank all of the people at Raku who have made this book and one of my dreams possible; all of the chefs, in particular David Tombs, Lynda Benko and Nobuko Kaji for their input and support; all of the serving staff who make Raku a one-of-a-kind dining experience; Akio Tsunashima for his wonderful photographs; Lynn Jennings, Janette Hooper and Elaine Jones for their help in polishing the manuscript; and my wife, Laurie Robertson, and family for giving me the time and support to do this project.

Contents

Introduction

*I*n this book, the flavors of the world are united in a style that has been described as Japanese tapas by some and Asian eclectic by others. It is a melting pot of ideas, styles and techniques that was born in the Northwest Territories and developed in Europe and Japan.

As a child growing up in the Northwest Territories, I was fortunate to be exposed to good cooking at a young age. This is somewhat remarkable considering the scarcity and poor quality of the ingredients available at that time. As my interest in cooking grew through my teens, cooking magazines became my prime source of inspiration and I longed to visit the exotic places and explore the evocative cuisines that I read about each month. Neither of these courses was open to me, so in true northern fashion I made do with what was available. I would choose a dish to cook, go down to the local Hudson's Bay store for groceries, and if I was lucky, I would find two of the ten required ingredients. For the rest I improvised. This gave me a good grounding in discovering which things worked together and which didn't. Even more important was the realization that traditional methods, while very good, were not the only ones available.

After I left the north, for the first time I could readily put my hands on most of the ingredients that the magazine recipes called for. I also had the opportunity to eat at ethnic restaurants and experience other interpretations of the dishes that made up my repertoire. It was at this time that I first discovered and fell in love with Japanese food—in particular, the Japanese style of presentation.

At a cooking school in London, I polished my skills as a cook and continued to explore the cuisines of the world. At the same time I met my wife, Laurie, who is also my business partner and a driving force behind our restaurant, Raku. We shared a mutual love of Japanese food and culture and decided to make that island nation our next stop. There we spent a glorious year, learning the mysteries of Japanese cooking and immersing ourselves in Japanese culture.

In Tokyo we were invited to a type of restaurant called an *izakaya*. It could best be described as a local pub where Japanese office workers went after a long day to drown their woes. What intrigued us about these establishments was the interesting selection of small dishes that accompanied the tankards of beer and *tokuri* of sake. The atmosphere was relaxing and convivial, but the emphasis was definitely on the liquor rather than the food.

Thus the idea of Raku was born: the food would be served izakaya-style, in small portions, allowing the diner to sample a wide selection of dishes. Like many diners, we had noticed the most interesting dishes in restaurants were often found in the appetizer section of the menu.

Rather than limiting the menu to Japanese cuisine, we decided to incorporate flavors from around the world. The Orange-Spiced Lamb Shanks are a good example of a dish that fits this concept. Braised lamb shanks, which have their origins in both French and Chinese cuisine, are simmered in a Chinese-style broth flavored with orange, cinnamon and soy sauce, crisped on the grill California-style, garnished with a French garlic aioli sauce and presented simply on a beautiful Japanese plate.

How to use this book

Despite the fact that I have provided exact measures and lists of ingredients for the recipes in this book, I have a strong belief that cooking is not, and should not be, an exact art. I am a cook of the dash, pinch and splash school of cooking. Food should be experienced with all of the senses; touch and hearing should be as important in the preparation stage as the senses of taste, sight and smell. I like to get my hands into the food, measure with my hands, judge doneness by feel, sound and smell. This takes experience, of course, but you will never acquire that experience if you don't experiment yourself. It doesn't really matter if the dish tastes exactly the same every time you make it; what is important is that it tastes good every time you make it!

The essence of this cooking style is improvisation. Don't be constrained by the written word, be inspired by it.

Some of the ingredients called for in this book are unusual, but they do make the food as unique as it is. Try to find the ingredients, but do not be afraid to try the alternatives suggested or make up your own substitutions. The dishes produced will be different but tasty nonetheless. The Pantry section on the following pages will help you stock many basic ingredients for making the recipes.

The organization of this book is also a little unorthodox, but logical in its own way. It is divided into sections, first by season and then by geographical orientation. Within each Looking East and Looking West section the recipes are organized into salads and or vegetables, seafood, fish, poultry and meat. The seasonal nature of the book is very important. If you turn to the summer section in the middle of summer you will have a good chance of finding a dish that appeals to you and a very good chance of finding all the ingredients called for.

All the recipes in this book are for four people except for the sushi recipes. The quantity of sushi rice made in the Wild Sushi section should make eight to ten rolls and each of the recipes for the various kinds of rolls are for one roll. This gives flexibility in choosing a variety of rolls to combine in a mixed sushi plate.

Please use this book as a guide to a style of cooking that I think brings the world closer together. Enjoy the flavors of different cuisines presented side by side. Enjoy the knowledge that the recipes are low in fat and for the most part easy to use. Enjoy the exploration of new and unfamiliar ingredients. Most importantly, enjoy the food!

The Pantry

*T*he pantry contains a guide to some of the more unusual and frequently used ingredients in the book. Once you have these things on hand you will find that the recipes are quick and simple to prepare. I have divided the pantry into two sections: fresh foods that will need to be used soon after purchase and nonperishables.

Fresh

Thai basil is a very fragrant member of the basil family. The Thais call it horapah basil and it is the most widely available of the several basils used in Thai cuisine. It has a purple stem with green leaves and often a bunch of small purple flowers, which are also edible. It has more of an anise flavor than standard basil, which can be used as a substitute.

Jalapeño chilies are probably the most widely available chilies in North America, due to their extensive use in Mexican food. They may be mild or spicy due to the wonders of genetic manipulation, and the only way to tell is to bite into one. Jalapeños are plump, triangular chilies and are either a deep green or a vivid red color. The green ones are always spicier than the red. You can substitute serrano or bird chilies for the jalapeños, but since jalapeños are the most widely available you will probably end up using these in place of all of the others.

Serrano chilies are the same color as jalapeños but are smaller and more slender. They are always spicy. They are readily available in most supermarkets. You can substitute jalapeños, but make sure you have the spicy ones!

Bird chilies are small, green and red chilies that look like the beak of a bird, hence the name. They are sometimes called Thai chilies because of their extensive use in Thai cuisine and have an intense, up-front heat that dissipates slowly. You can substitute jalapeño or serrano chilies, but use more if you want to experience the true heat intensity.

Anaheim chilies are long, slender, mild green and red chilies. Very popular in the southern United States, they are available in Mexican groceries and most supermarkets. If you can't find them, use green and red bell peppers instead.

Ginger is one of the most indispensable ingredients in Asian cookery. There is not a single cuisine in the East that does not use it. It is a wonderful flavor, at the same time spicy and cool. Luckily it is very easy to find, being available in most supermarkets and all Asian markets. To peel or not to peel? The skin of fresh ginger is very thin and does not detract from the dish in any way. I do not bother to peel ginger, preferring to wash it and use peel and all. The only exception to this is if the brown color of the skin will mar the final appearance of the dish.

Kaffir limes are the small, wrinkled, wild limes of Southeast Asia and can often be found in Thai markets. They are exquisitely aromatic and add a wonderful complexity to any dish in which they are used. The zest is the most important part of the kaffir lime, the juice being scarce and the number of seeds prodigious. Substitute regular lime juice if you can't lay your hands on some kaffir limes.

Kaffir lime leaves are the leaves of the kaffir lime tree. They also can be found in the refrigerator section of Southeast Asian markets. They have an incredible aroma, slightly more delicate than the limes, and can be used in large quantities without being bitter, unlike kaffir lime peel. They are usually sold on the branches, which have wicked thorns, and are easily recognized because it looks like one leaf is growing out of the end of the other. The flavor is not easily replaced, but you can use the zest and juice of a regular lime in a pinch.

My favorite type of **salmon** is spring, also known as chinook or king; it has a pink-orange color and a delicate texture. Very close in texture and color is the Atlantic salmon. Many people prefer the brilliant red color and robust flavor of sockeye salmon. Pink and chum salmon are also tasty but a little coarser in texture and light pink in color. Use any of these varieties in the dishes in this book. When you use raw salmon, make sure that it has been previously frozen. Freezing the fish kills any parasites that may have been present.

Tuna comes in three main varieties: albacore, which has pale soft meat and is the favorite of people in the northwest; yellowfin, or 'ahi, which comes from Hawaii and has a deep red color and a beeflike texture when raw; and bluefin, which is so highly prized in Japan that we rarely see it in North America. All are acceptable for use in the recipes in this book. A good place to find tuna and many other Japanese ingredients is from the wholesalers who supply sushi restaurants. They usually cater, on a retail basis, to the Japanese community. Drop by the warehouse to see if this is the case. If fresh or frozen tuna is not available, many of the recipes will work with salmon.

Fresh **water chestnuts**, sometimes available at Oriental markets, have a brown shiny skin that makes them look a lot like regular chestnuts. The skin is very thin and easily peeled, revealing the crisp, sweet, white flesh. Canned water chestnuts will provide the crunch, if not the flavor, of the fresh and are available in many supermarkets.

Nonperishable

Ancho chilies are one of a plethora of chilies used in Mexican cuisine. They are dried, black and large, and they have a wonderful, smoky, tea-like flavor and a moderate heat quotient. They are available at all Mexican groceries. If you can't find them, use an equal weight of Mexican chili powder in the recipe.

Chili paste with garlic is found in just about every Asian cuisine. It varies in spiciness, ranging from very spicy to volcanic! I am a big fan of the Vietnamese version. It can be found in Asian markets or the Asian section at your supermarket.

Chinese fermented black beans are black beans that have been cooked, salted, fermented and dried. They are used in the southern provinces of China in much the same way that Parmesan cheese is used in Italy. They add an extra dimension to a dish and are something that should be a permanent fixture in your pantry. You

can find them in all Chinese groceries and at most supermarkets these days.

Thai **fish sauce** is used by Southeast Asian cultures in much the same way that Chinese culture uses soy sauce, to add salt and complexity to a dish. Fish sauce is made by layering anchovies and salt in wooden or stone barrels and fermenting them in the sun for several weeks. The resulting liquid is siphoned off and bottled for use. Different cultures use different fish as the base and you will sometimes see shrimp sauce. The smell and taste of this sauce on its own can be off-putting to the first-time user, but it adds a wonderful richness and sophistication to any dish in which it is used. The same process is used to make shrimp paste, one of the staples of Indonesian and Malay cookery. Fish sauce can substitute for shrimp paste and if you really need to, you can use soy sauce instead of fish sauce. Be warned that soy sauce will color the dish, whereas the fish sauce will not. Fish sauce and shrimp paste are available in Southeast Asian markets and some supermarkets.

Thai **fried garlic** is an indispensable garnish for many foods. It, along with Thai fried onions or shallots, is available in Southeast Asian and Indian markets. Both are crisply fried to a deep nutty brown with a wonderful rich flavor. You will find yourself sprinkling them on everything in sight!

The **pickled ginger,** or *gari,* is the kind that you get at sushi bars to accompany your sushi. It comes in two colors, pink and natural. The pink has been tinted with a food coloring so I prefer not to use it. It is available at Japanese markets and also at a lot of supermarkets. If you are having trouble finding it go to your local sushi bar; they will be able to help you out.

Pickled ginger juice, is the pickling liquid that the pickled ginger comes in.

Hoisin sauce is sometimes called Chinese barbecue sauce. It is sweet and slightly spicy and is traditionally used for the pancake and crisp skin course of Peking duck. One of many sauces based on fermented soybeans, it is readily available in all Chinese groceries and most supermarkets.

Mirin is a sweet rice wine that is used extensively in Japanese cooking. It is available in Japanese groceries and in some supermarkets and health food stores. You can substitute an equivalent amount of sugar or some sweet sherry.

Miso is a fermented soybean paste popular in Japan and to a lesser extent in other northern Asian cultures. It comes in a variety of types, the most common being white, red and dark. White miso is sweeter than the others and is the favorite of the people of imperial Kyoto in Japan. Red miso is the everyday miso of Japan and is used for many things. It is much saltier and the flavor more robust than white miso; a little goes a long way. Dark miso is not used as extensively because it is very strong, but if you mix a little dark miso with some of the red to make the base for a winter stew or soup, there are few things more satisfying. Miso is available in all Japanese food stores and in

all health food stores. The miso in health food stores have different names, so you will have to try them or go by the color to get the one you want. There is no real substitute for miso, although the Chinese use different kinds of bean paste, and in a pinch you can try those.

Red **mustard seeds** are a staple of Indian cookery and can be found in any Indian market. The yellow mustard seeds, more commonly available, are a fine substitute.

Bean thread noodles are sometimes called Chinese vermicelli, glass or cellophane noodles, or *harusame*. They are thin wiry noodles made from mung bean flour. With not a lot of taste of their own, these noodles are used mostly as a textural backdrop in many dishes. They resemble thin rice noodles, so check the ingredients on the package before buying. These noodles also make an interesting garnish. When tossed into hot oil they puff up into crunchy, white sticks which can be used on top of salads, curries or stir-fries. They are available in Chinese markets and almost all supermarkets these days. You can substitute any very thin noodle.

Rice noodles come in a huge variety of sizes, ranging from vermicelli to sheets the size of lasagna noodles. Most Chinese groceries will carry a selection of fresh rice noodles in the refrigerator section as well as shelf upon shelf of the dried. Rice noodles have a distinctive flavor, but pasta can be used in their stead.

Somen noodles are Japanese wheat flour vermicelli-style noodles. In Japan, this is a summertime favorite that is served cold in ice water with a soy dipping sauce. Some fancier places even have the somen flowing in bamboo pipes past the diners, who scoop out some noodles at their leisure. Somen comes packaged in pretty little bundles, generally five to a package. They are available at Japanese markets and health food shops. Use any wheat flour vermicelli-style noodle as a substitute.

Szechuan peppercorns are the seeds of the prickly ash tree. They are dried and ground for seasoning in Chinese cooking. The Japanese call the powder *sancho* and the two can be used interchangeably. It is the secret ingredient used by Japanese restaurants on their grilled dishes and when sprinkled on food adds an intriguing citrusy tang. Lemon pepper is a passable substitute. You can find these peppercorns in all Chinese and Japanese markets.

Sancho pepper (*see* Szechuan peppercorns).

Shrimp paste (*see* Thai fish sauce).

Tamarind purée or tamarind concentrate can be found in Indian groceries and in some Asian markets. It is the refined pulp of the tamarind fruit and is used extensively in Southeast Asia to add a sour component to a dish. Balsamic vinegar makes a great substitute.

Tofu, or bean curd, is a mainstay of Asian cooking. It comes in many different varieties, a few of which we use in this book. Tofu puffs are pieces of tofu that have been deep-fried until all of the moisture in the tofu is gone. This leaves a brown, puffy pillow that is usually parboiled and squeezed to get rid of excess oil, then either stuffed or shredded and used in soups and stir-fries. Flavored dried tofu is firm tofu that has been air-dried and marinated in a soy-based marinade. Both are readily available at Asian markets, health food stores, and some supermarkets.

Chinese black vinegar is readily available in Chinese markets. It is made from wheat, millet or sorghum and flavored with cassia bark and star anise. You can substitute balsamic vinegar.

Chinese red vinegar is readily available in Chinese grocery stores. You can substitute red wine vinegar. Experiment a bit with the different vinegars that are out there. The range is amazing and the different flavor combinations are infinite.

Rice wine vinegar can be found in almost all Asian cultures. The kind I generally use is the Japanese variety. You can buy sushi vinegar that is already prepared for making sushi, but don't substitute regular rice vinegar, as it is quite sweet.

Umeboshi vinegar is the tart liquid left after the manufacture of Japanese pickled plums. It is salty, intensely flavored and colored red with shiso, the fragrant leaves of the perilla plant. It can be found at health food and Japanese specialty stores.

Spring

Growing up in the Northwest Territories, in the far north of Canada, I think one develops a skewed idea of what seasons mean. As we endured minus 40° temperatures and blizzards in March, it was always interesting to read about and watch spring unfold in books, in magazines and on television. When it finally arrived in Fort Smith, it seemed to be only about one week long. The snow would melt, the ditches would be swollen with water, the trees would burst into leaf—all in a terrible hurry. Farther south the seasons progress at a much more leisurely pace. The common element, however, is the smell, feel and excitement in the air of renewed life. This feeling pushes me to be on the lookout for things I haven't seen for a while: vegetables that have bright fresh flavors and colors; lighter, more delicately flavored fish and meat; and light, bright and simple sauces.

Spring

Looking East

Eyes go one way;

nose goes another;

and flowers come in spring.

-Author unknown

Calamari Salad with Black Beans and Ginger

This is a tasty, relatively fat-free way to prepare calamari. It is lightly blanched to give just a slight crunch to the meat without transforming it into rubber bands. You can find cleaned squid tubes and tentacles in the frozen section of many Chinese groceries, supermarkets and fishmongers. If you can only find whole uncleaned squid, don't despair— just get a little dirty and clean them yourself (this is a favorite activity of my four-year-old daughter, who loves to help dad cook). This recipe makes more dressing than you need for the salad, but once you taste it you will be using it on everything, I promise!

Serving Suggestion

Combines well with Chicken with Sweet Chili Sauce (page 25) and Grilled Shiitake Mushrooms with Ponzu (page 20).

Make the ginger vinaigrette.

Combine in the bowl of a food processor and process until smooth:

2 serrano chilies, stem removed*
2 cloves garlic
1 Tbsp. (15 ml) grated fresh ginger
3/4 cup (185 ml) pickled ginger*
1 tsp. (5 ml) chili paste with garlic*
2/3 cup (160 ml) cilantro leaves
3 Tbsp. (45 ml) pickled ginger juice*
1 tsp. (5 ml) apple cider vinegar
3/4 cup (185 ml) vegetable oil

Slice into rings:
1 lb. (450 g) cleaned calamari

If you are going to clean the calamari yourself, the procedure is very simple, but a little messy. Start by pulling the head off the body of the squid. Cut the tentacles off the head, just in front of the eyes. Reserve the tentacles and discard the head and any insides attached to it. Pull the cartilage, which looks a bit like a clear plastic feather, out of the body and discard. Squeeze the body like a tube of toothpaste from the closed end to the open, to remove any remaining innards.

Reserve the bodies. When you are finished cleaning, cut the bodies into rings.

Bring a large saucepan of water to a full boil, then add the calamari. Remove from the heat. Let the calamari sit in the water for 1 minute. It is cooked when it turns pink and the edges of the rings start to curl. Drain the calamari and immerse in cold water to stop the cooking process. Drain and set aside.

Finely dice:
1/2 red bell pepper
1/2 yellow bell pepper
1/4 small red onion

Toss the calamari with 1/2 cup (125 ml) of the vinaigrette and mix with the peppers and onions.

Divide among 4 plates:
4 cups (1 l) mixed baby lettuce

Arrange 1/4 of the calamari mixture on top of each serving of lettuce. Sprinkle with:
2 Tbsp. (30 ml) Chinese fermented black beans, chopped*

* See The Pantry

Shrimp and Bamboo Salad

This salad, with its hot, pungent, fragrant Thai ingredients, is typical of Thailand and a refreshing addition to any Asian meal. The bird chilies are very hot, so be brave—or not, and leave them out! You can substitute fresh cooked crabmeat for the rock shrimp. For something a little fruitier without the crunch, try julienned mango instead of the bamboo shoots.

Make the lime dressing.

Combine:

juice of 1 lime (about 2 Tbsp./ 30 ml)
1 Tbsp. (15 ml) red wine vinegar
2 Tbsp. (30 ml) olive oil
1 clove garlic, minced
4 bird chilies, minced*
2 green onions, minced
3 sprigs mint, coarsely chopped
1/2 tsp. (2.5 ml) Thai fish sauce*

Set aside.

Bring a pot of water to a boil with:

1 tsp. (5 ml) salt

Add:

1/2 lb. (225 g) Florida rock shrimp

Turn off the heat and let the shrimp sit in the water for 1 minute. Drain and immerse the shrimp in cold water to stop the cooking process. Drain.

Combine the shrimp with:

1/4 red bell pepper, finely diced
1/4 yellow bell pepper, finely diced
1 cup (250 ml) julienned bamboo shoots

Toss the shrimp and vegetables with the lime dressing.

Divide among 4 plates:

4 cups (1 l) salad greens

Top with the shrimp and bamboo mixture.

Garnish with:

4 sprigs cilantro

*See The Pantry

Serving Suggestion

Combines well with New Potatoes in Parchment (page 35) and Chicken with Prickly Pear Sauce (page 40).

Note on Ingredients

Bamboo shoots are readily available in the can; however, a much better version is available frozen in plastic bags. The frozen ones have a wonderful fresh flavor and texture that the canned ones can't match. The bamboo shoots can be found in most Asian markets that carry Thai and Chinese ingredients.

Florida rock shrimp are small shrimp that are sold peeled and deveined. They are sweet and crunchy when cooked. If you cannot find them substitute spot or tiger prawns, but they must be peeled and deveined after cooking.

Tea-Smoked Prawn and Shiso Salad

I have always been intrigued by the thought of smoking food to impart flavor as opposed to preserving the food. While living in the Northwest Territories I came across a recipe for tea-smoked duck. When we tried it we found out that normal kitchen ventilation is not up to the task of evacuating huge amounts of smoke. My suggestion is to use your outside barbecue for this dish, but if you want to use the traditional method and feel that your fan can cope with the smoke, by all means try it.

In a bowl combine:

4 cups (1 l) water
3/4 cup (185 ml) sugar
1/2 cup (125 ml) salt
1 Tbsp. (15 ml) 5-spice powder
1 Tbsp. (15 ml) crushed Szechuan peppercorns*
1 Tbsp. (15 ml) coarsely ground black pepper
24 large spot prawns in the shell (or any large fresh prawns)

Marinate the mixture for 1/2 hour. While the prawns are marinating, make the salad dressing.

Mix:

2 Tbsp. (30 ml) umeboshi vinegar*
1 Tbsp. (15 ml) soy sauce
1 tsp. (5 ml) sugar

Set aside the dressing.

Remove the prawns from the marinade and put into a steamer or bowl.

If you are using the barbecue to smoke the prawns, preheat it to hot. Put a double piece of foil on the coals or stones.

Add:

3 Tbsp. (45 ml) tea leaves of your choice (I like lychee tea)
3 Tbsp. (45 ml) raw rice
3 Tbsp. (45 ml) wood shavings (cedar, hickory and oak are all nice)
1 Tbsp. (15 ml) sugar

When the mixture is smoking, place the bowl or steamer containing the prawns onto the barbecue rack and close the lid. Smoke for 5-10 minutes, or until the prawns are just cooked.

If you are using the traditional method to smoke the prawns, line an old wok or pot with 2 layers of tin foil. Add the tea mixture (see above). Heat the wok until the ingredients are smoking. Put 2 chopsticks into the wok to keep the bowl above the smoking tea

Note on Ingredients

Shiso leaves are the leaves of the perilla plant. They come in both green and red and have a wonderful flavor. You can find them at Japanese groceries and, if you must, can substitute basil.

Five-spice powder is a common Chinese seasoning featuring cinnamon, star anise, Szechuan peppercorns, fennel and cloves. It is found in all supermarkets.

mixture. Set the bowl or steamer into the wok and cover tightly with foil and a lid. Smoke 5-10 minutes, or until the prawns are just cooked.

Arrange:

4 handfuls mixed salad greens
4 shiso leaves, shredded

on 4 plates, with the shiso on top. Dress with a little of the vinaigrette. Peel the prawns and arrange 6 on each plate. You may serve the prawns in their shells and let people peel them at the table for a more intense flavor.

*See The Pantry

Variation: A simple version of this dish uses a Japanese barbecued eel called *unagi kaba yaki*, available at all Japanese markets. This delicacy is precooked and only has to be warmed up under the broiler before being put on top of the salad.

Serving Suggestion

Combines well with Taro Pancakes with Spicy Tuna (page 38) and Hot and Sour Baby Bok Choy (page 34).

Green Lip Mussel Salad

This salad is a variation of Japanese sunomono, which translates literally as "vinegared things." Sunomono salads usually feature some kind of seafood and harusame noodles (bean thread vermicelli). This recipe works well with any kind of mussel or clam.

Serving Suggestion

Combines well with Crab Potstickers (page 23) and Yaki Onigiri (page141).

Make the Vietnamese salad dressing.

Combine in a food processor or a mortar:

1 jalapeño chili, minced*
1 clove garlic, minced
2 Tbsp. (30 ml) sugar

Process or grind with a pestle until the mixture is relatively smooth. Add:

1/2 cup (125 ml) Thai fish sauce*
juice of 1 lime
zest and juice of 1 kaffir lime*

Stir to combine.

Cover the bottom of a saucepan with 1/2" (1 cm) of water. Add:

16 New Zealand green lip mussels

Cover and boil 2-3 minutes, or until the mussels open. Remove from the pan and cool. Remove the top shell from the mussel so that the meat is lying on the bottom shell.

Bring another small saucepan of water to a boil. Add:

1-oz. (30-g) package bean thread noodles*

Simmer 2 minutes, or until the noodles are soft but still slightly firm. Drain in a strainer. Refresh under cold running water to stop the cooking process.

Toss the noodles with a little of the dressing and arrange small mounds on 4 plates. Place 4 mussels on top of each pile of noodles and drizzle a little of the dressing into each mussel.

Garnish with:

4 sprigs Thai basil*

*See The Pantry

Note on Ingredients

New Zealand green lip mussels are, after lamb and kiwis, one of New Zealand's most important food exports. They are about twice as big as our native black mussels and the shells are a beautiful iridescent green with a pearly white interior. They make gorgeous hors d'oeuvres. If you can't find fresh, they are available frozen and precooked on the half-shell.

Tofu and Vegetable Packages

When Laurie and I were in Japan we tried inari sushi—sweetened tofu puffs filled with sushi rice— for the first time. It became an instant favorite; in fact, by the time we left Japan it was the only kind of sushi that Laurie could still bring herself to eat. I wanted to use the tofu puffs in another way, so we developed this recipe. Baby corn, peas, green soy beans and mochi (see page 104) all make good stuffing ingredients.

Note on Ingredients

Bottled teriyaki sauce may be substituted for the homemade tare yaki sauce with some sacrifice in flavor. You can make the bottled sauce a little more interesting by boiling it with a piece of ginger, a couple of cloves of garlic, some leek and an apple for 20 minutes or so. Strain it and put it back in the bottle.

There are many brands of **soy sauce** on the market. I generally prefer to use the Japanese brands as they have a fresh-brewed quality. The Chinese brands are a little saltier and coarser in flavor. I use dark or regular soy sauce in most recipes except where noted. The other two types of soy sauce used in the book are tamari and mushroom. Tamari is a less refined version of soy sauce; it does not have any wheat added to it in the brewing process, making it a good choice for people with allergies to wheat. Mushroom soy is a Chinese soy sauce that has been reduced with dried black mushrooms to give it a characteristic flavor. It is very dark and strong and should be used cautiously.

Make the tare yaki sauce.

Combine in a medium pot:

2 1/2 cups (625 ml) sake
1 1/2 cups (375 ml) mirin*
2 cups (500 ml) brown sugar
4 cups (1 l) Japanese soy sauce
1/2 cup (125 ml) tamari soy sauce
1 small onion, chopped
4 cloves garlic, chopped
2" (5-cm) piece fresh ginger, chopped
1 small apple, chopped
1 orange, chopped, skin on
1 small pear, chopped
1 small leek, chopped

Bring everything to a boil and cook until the mixture is reduced by 20 percent. Strain into a large jar. The sauce will keep in the fridge for 3 months.

Bring a large pot of water to the boil. Open:

1 package deep-fried tofu puffs (6-8 puffs)*

Put the puffs into the boiling water and cover with a lid that is slightly smaller than the pot to make sure they are submerged. Boil for 10 minutes. This removes excess oil from the puffs. Drain the puffs and let them cool.

Assemble the following ingredients:

1 large carrot, peeled, cut into 2" (5-cm) lengths and julienned
1 piece flavored dried tofu, cut into 1" (2.5-cm) squares*
8 fresh water chestnuts, peeled*
1 green onion, cut into 2" (5-cm) lengths

Bring a small pan of water to a boil and blanch the carrots until crisp-tender, about 4 minutes. Drain and run under cold water to cool.

With a knife or pair of scissors, cut a slit along one edge of each tofu puff. Work your finger into the slit until you have a small pouch, taking care not to rip the sides or bottom of the puff.

Divide the assembled ingredients equally among the tofu puffs and stuff them.

Heat your barbecue to medium-high or turn on the oven broiler and adjust the rack to 6" (15 cm) below the heat. Grill or broil the packages for 4 minutes on each side.

Fill a small bowl with the tare yaki sauce.

Dip the cooked packages into the tare yaki sauce. Drain the excess and put them onto a serving plate.

Sprinkle with a little:
sancho pepper*

*See The Pantry

Serving Suggestion

Combines well with Polynesian 'Ahi Salad (page 28) and Thai Crab Cakes (page 22).

*Artichoke with Ginger
Vinaigrette, page 33*

Chrysanthemum Greens with
Sesame Dressing, page 19

Chrysanthemum Greens with Sesame Dressing

People are very fond of ohitashi (vegetables tossed with a sesame-based dressing) at Japanese restaurants. Spinach is the most common vegetable to be treated in this way, but the Japanese like to do ohitashi with almost every green imaginable. When I was in Japan I tried ohitashi made with pea tips, garlic chives and the chrysanthemum leaves that I am using here. The point is, don't be afraid to substitute just about any green vegetable that you want for the chrysanthemum greens.

Make the dressing.

Grind in a mortar or process in a food processor:

1/2 cup (125 ml) toasted sesame seeds

Add:

1/2 cup (125 ml) dashi soup stock (see page 121)
1 tsp. (5 ml) mirin*
1 Tbsp. (15 ml) soy sauce
pinch salt

Wash and trim:

1 bunch chrysanthemum greens

Bring a pot of water to a boil. Plunge the greens into the boiling water for about 30 seconds. Remove them from the hot water and immediately plunge them into cold water to stop the cooking process and fix their color. Remove them from the water and squeeze out excess liquid.

Toss the greens with the dressing, cover and place in the fridge for a couple of hours. Divide the greens among 4 bowls and pour any remaining sauce over them. Top them with a sprinkle of:

sesame seeds

*See The Pantry

Serving Suggestion

Combines well with Shrimp and Bamboo Happy Cakes (page 21) and Asparagus with Mustard Butter (page 32).

Note on Ingredients

Chrysanthemum greens are the edible leaves of the chrysanthemum flower. The ones in this recipe are slightly different from the flowers that you grow at home but those are also edible. You can find them in Japanese markets where they are called *kikuna* or *shingiku*. The Chinese call them *chung ho*. This is a spring vegetable.

Grilled Shiitake Mushrooms with Ponzu Sauce

I know, I know, mushrooms are a fall and winter thing, but wonderful cultivated shiitake mushrooms are rapidly becoming available all year round, so check your local supermarket. If you can't get shiitake mushrooms, even the humble button mushroom is delicious done in this way. The lime juice in the sauce lightens the flavor of the mushrooms, making them a great addition to a spring barbecue. When you grill these or any mushrooms, remember that they shrink quite dramatically when cooked, so choose the biggest you can find.

Make the ponzu sauce.

Combine in a bowl:

1 cup (250 ml) soy sauce
1/4 cup (60 ml) lime juice

Stir to mix.

Preheat the barbecue grill to medium or turn on the oven broiler and adjust the rack to 3" (7.5 cm) below the heat.

Cut the stems off:

**16 very large Shiitake
    mushrooms**

You can reserve the stems to add to chicken stock or tare yaki sauce (see page 18). Brush the mushrooms with a little:

vegetable oil

Arrange the mushrooms cap side down on the grill or oven rack. Cook 3-4 minutes, or until a few drops of moisture appear on the mushrooms. Flip them over and cook 2 minutes longer. Remove from the heat.

Arrange on 4 plates. Drizzle with a little ponzu sauce. To finish, sprinkle with a little:

sancho pepper*

*See The Pantry

Serving Suggestion

Combines well with Calamari Salad with Black Beans and Ginger (page 12) and Chicken with Sweet Chili Sauce (page 25).

Note on Ingredients

Shiitake mushrooms are one of the treasures of Asian cuisine. They are used most extensively in their dried form in most cultures, but the Japanese are especially fond of them grilled fresh. They are sometimes known as black mushrooms. You can find them in health food stores that have a fresh produce section and at many supermarkets.

Shrimp and Bamboo Happy Cakes

I have always liked the concept of turning one meal into two or three. The classic example is Beef Daube, served hot the first night, en gelée for lunch the second and as a filling for ravioli the third. In this same way you can use leftover Shrimp and Bamboo Salad as the filling in this recipe for a Korean-style pancake.

Make one recipe of:
Shrimp and Bamboo Salad (page 13)

Preheat the oven to 250°F (120°C).

Combine in a measuring cup:
4 eggs
1 cup (250 ml) flour
pinch of salt

Mix until smooth.

Heat an 8" (20-cm) nonstick skillet over high heat for about 1 minute. Add:
1 tsp. (5 ml) sesame oil

Heat for a further 30 seconds, then pour in 1/4 of the batter and swirl the pan so the batter coats the bottom. Turn the heat to low. Put 1/4 of the salad onto the bottom half of the pancake. Fold the top half of the pancake over the salad. Remove from the pan and keep warm in the oven while you make the other 3 pancakes. Serve on individual plates.

Serving Suggestion

Combines well with Chrysanthemum Greens with Sesame Dressing (page 19) and Asparagus with Mustard Butter (page 32).

Thai Crab Cakes

Crab cakes are always popular no matter what form they take, but these are unique because they combine Thai herbs with Dungeness crabmeat for a wonderfully aromatic dish. These cakes are relatively expensive because they are almost all crab and no filler, but they are well worth it!

Combine in a bowl:

1 1/2 lbs. (675 g) lump crabmeat

1/2 cup (125 ml) fine dry breadcrumbs

2 eggs

1 tsp. (5 ml) Vietnamese chili paste with garlic*

1 Tbsp. (15 ml) finely minced kaffir lime leaf*

1 jalapeño chili, finely minced*

2 green onions, sliced

1 tsp. (5 ml) Thai fish sauce*

Mix the ingredients thoroughly. Form the mixture into small cakes 1 1/2" (4 cm) in diameter. You should have about 12 crab cakes.

Make a colorful pepper salsa to garnish the crab cakes. Combine in a small bowl:

1/2 small red bell pepper, very finely diced

1/2 small yellow bell pepper, very finely diced

1 jalapeño chili, finely minced*

zest of one lime

1/2 tsp. (2.5 ml) finely minced kaffir lime leaf*

1 tsp. (5 ml) Thai fish sauce*

Heat:

1 Tbsp. (15 ml) butter

in a nonstick skillet over medium-high heat. Sauté the crab cakes until heated through and brown on both sides. Remove to four plates and garnish with the pepper salsa.

*See The Pantry

Serving Suggestion

Combines well with Korean Spiced Tuna (page 100) and Artichokes with Ginger Vinaigrette (page 33).

Crab Potstickers

Potstickers, sometimes known as gyoza, are always a favorite. They can also be fun to make. My four-year-old daughter, D'Laine, likes to help put them together, but she likes eating them even more. Gyoza wrappers are round and thicker than wonton skins. They are found in all Asian markets and in many super-markets. Using crab for the filling is a little extravagant, but well worth it every now and then.

This recipe makes quite a few dumplings; however, they freeze very well. To freeze, arrange the dumplings on a cookie sheet lined with plastic wrap, and put them in your freezer overnight. Remove them from the cookie sheet and store them in plastic freezer bags. Use them straight from the freezer.

Serving Suggestion

Combines well with Korean Spiced Tuna (page 100) and Artichokes with Ginger Vinaigrette (page 33).

Make the crab filling.

Combine in a bowl:
1 1/2 lbs. (675 g) lump crabmeat
1/2 cup (125 ml) fine dry breadcrumbs
2 eggs
1 tsp. (5 ml) Vietnamese chili paste with garlic*
1 jalapeño chili, finely minced*
1/2 small red bell pepper, very finely diced
1/2 small yellow bell pepper, very finely diced
2 green onions, sliced
1 Tbsp. (15 ml) Thai fish sauce*

Make the dipping sauce.

Combine in a food processor or a mortar:
1 jalapeño chili, minced*
1 clove garlic, minced
2 Tbsp. (30 ml) sugar

Process or grind until the mixture is relatively smooth.

Add:
1/2 cup (125 ml) Thai fish sauce*
juice of 1 lime
zest and juice of 1 kaffir lime*

Stir to combine and set aside.

Set out a bowl of water to wet the edges of the potstickers.

Open a package of:
gyoza wrappers

Take one wrapper out of the package. Place a small spoonful of the filling on the center of the wrapper. Dip your finger in the water and run it around the edge of the wrapper. Fold the wrapper over, enclosing the filling in a crescent-shaped dumpling. Squeeze the edges together to seal. Set the potsticker on a plate and repeat the procedure until all of the filling has been used.

To cook the potstickers, heat a sauté pan until very hot with:
3 Tbsp. (45 ml) vegetable oil

Add 12 potstickers to the pan and cook them until they are brown and crisp on one side. Add 1/2 cup (125 ml) of water. Reduce the heat to low and put a lid on the pan. Cook for another 2-3 minutes, or until you can hear them sizzling in the oil again. Remove to 4 plates and serve with a small bowl of the dipping sauce.

*See The Pantry

Scallops with Spicy Miso

We are finally starting to see whole scallops in the shell. This is a great thing for the consumer because it opens up the possibility of using the whole scallop, as they do in most other cultures, instead of just the frozen-at-sea adductor muscles. If you are having a hard time finding Chinese greens for this dish, use spinach.

Make the miso sauce.

Combine in a bowl:

4 Tbsp. (60 ml) white miso*
1 Tbsp. (15 ml) mirin*
1 Tbsp. (15 ml) rice wine vinegar*
1 tsp. (5 ml) sugar
1 tsp. (5 ml) Vietnamese chili paste with garlic*

Set aside.

Trim the woody ends off:
8 pieces of Chinese greens, preferably *yu choy sum*

Rinse and set aside.

Thread:
24 large scallops
on bamboo skewers, 3 per skewer.

Preheat your barbecue grill to medium-high or turn on the oven broiler and adjust the rack to 6" (15 cm) below the heat. Barbecue or broil the skewers for 2-3 minutes on each side or until just done. Do not overcook the scallops, which can become tough and lose a lot of flavor when cooked too long.

Steam the greens until crisp-tender. You can tell if the greens are done by looking at the stem end. There will be a white dot in the middle of the stalk if not quite ready. When they are done the white spot will have vanished.

Divide the greens among 4 plates. Cut them in half. Arrange the skewers on top of the greens. Drizzle some of the miso sauce onto each skewer.

*See The Pantry

Serving Suggestion

Combines well with Korean Spiced Tuna (page 100) and Artichokes with Ginger Vinaigrette (page 33).

Chicken with Sweet Chili Sauce

This chicken dish is a typical snack food of northern Thailand, and it always evokes the rain forest for me. Perhaps it is the sweetness of the chili sauce mingled with the smokiness of the sesame oil and the barbecue.

Make the marinade.

In a flat bowl that will hold the chicken skewers, combine:

1 1/2 cups (375 ml) sweet chili sauce for chicken

1 clove garlic, minced

1 Tbsp. (15 ml) chili paste with garlic*

1 Tbsp. (15 ml) hoisin sauce*

1 Tbsp. (15 ml) sesame oil

1 Tbsp. (15 ml) toasted sesame seeds

Cut into 1" (2.5-cm) cubes:

4 skinless chicken breasts or 6 boneless thighs

Thread the chicken on 8-12 bamboo skewers. Marinate the chicken skewers in 1 cup (250 ml) of the sweet chili marinade for at least 30 minutes. Reserve the remaining marinade for basting the chicken.

Preheat the barbecue grill to medium or turn on the oven broiler and adjust the rack to 6" (15 cm) beneath the heat. Shake the excess marinade off the skewers and barbecue or broil them for 3-5 minutes on each side, or until thoroughly cooked. The marinade is sweet, so watch that the chicken doesn't burn.

*See The Pantry

Serving Suggestion

Combines well with Hot and Sour Baby Bok Choy (page 34) and Yaki Onigiri (page 141).

Note on Ingredients

Sweet chili sauce for chicken is just that. It is not very spicy and is enormously popular as a dip for barbecue meats. It can be found at Asian markets or in the Asian section at your supermarket.

Spring

Looking West

Through the snow

the crocus

yearns for spring.

Polynesian 'Ahi Salad

This dish was inspired by a staff member's holiday in Hawaii. Yellowfin tuna, or 'ahi, is very popular in all of the Polynesian Islands. In the original version the tuna was cured seviche-style in a coconut milk-based sauce. This essentially cooks the tuna, toughening the proteins in the flesh. We thought it was a shame to lose the wonderful flavor and texture of the raw tuna and produced this variation. We use a coconut milk dressing for the salad and add it just before the salad is served. The vegetables in this dish may seem a little offbeat, but the key is to choose some fresh, crisp-textured vegetables that will contrast with the softness of the tuna. Substitute regular radishes and carrots if you can't get the jicama and daikon radish.

Make the dressing.

Combine in a food processor or a mortar:

1 jalapeño chili, minced*
1 clove garlic, minced
2 Tbsp. (30 ml) sugar

Process or grind with a pestle until the mixture is relatively smooth and liquid.

Add:

1/4 cup (60 ml) Thai fish sauce*
1/2 cup (125 ml) coconut milk
juice of 1 lime
zest and juice of 1 kaffir lime*

Stir to combine.

Prepare the vegetable salad.

Combine in a bowl:

3/4 cup (185 ml) jicama, peeled and cut into very fine dice
3/4 cup (185 ml) daikon radish, peeled and cut into very fine dice
3/4 cup (185 ml) fennel, cut into very fine dice
1/4 cup (60 ml) red bell pepper, cut into very fine dice
1/4 cup (60 ml) yellow bell pepper, cut into very fine dice

Toss the vegetables with 1/2 cup (125 ml) of the dressing.

Slice thinly:

1/2 lb. (225 g) 'ahi (yellowfin tuna)*

Divide the vegetables among 4 plates. Mound them into a dome shape. Cover the vegetables with slices of tuna. Drizzle some dressing over the tuna.

*See The Pantry

Serving Suggestion

Combines well with Thai Crab Cakes (page 22) and Tofu and Vegetable Packages (page 17).

Exotic Vegetable Chips

This is an interesting but optional garnish for the Polynesian 'Ahi Salad and for many other dishes. You can buy many of these exotic vegetable chips in bags at Oriental and Latin American markets and in some health food markets. Plain potato chips make a less interesting but passable substitute. It is important when deep-frying to bring the oil to the proper temperature. If you do not, the results will be uneven and disappointing.

Peel and slice very thinly any of the following vegetables:

taro root

yucca

lotus root

green plantain

In a saucepan, heat to 350°F (175°C).

1″ (2.5 cm) vegetable oil

When the oil is hot, add a few chips at a time and fry until they are very pale brown, then turn them over. Be sure to take them out before they get too brown, as they will continue to brown even after they have been removed from the oil. Drain on paper towel until cool. You may also use a deep fryer for this dish.

Note on Ingredients

Yucca, also known as cassava or manioc, is one of the most popular starchy tubers in the tropical world. It originated in Brazil, where it is used extensively. It can be prepared any way potatoes can and makes an interesting change.

Plantains, a starchy version of banana, are used in soups and stews throughout the Caribbean and Africa. They make great chips and fritters. Buy them green: they are difficult to peel but the ripe yellow ones are too mushy to slice well.

Lotus root is the vegetable that looks like a giant link of sausages. It is starchy and should be cooked with lemon juice or vinegar added to the cooking water to preserve its whiteness. It makes attractive chips because of the holes in each slice.

Taros are starchy tubers that look a little like striped hairy potatoes. They range in size from those as small as a walnut to giants about a foot (30 cm) long. They are popular all over the world, especially in the southern hemisphere. All of these vegetables can be found in Asian and Latin American markets.

Snap Peas with Grapefruit and Almonds

Snap peas are wonderful! As a child it seemed so novel to be able to pick them right off the bush and eat them shell and all. This recipe makes many more almonds than you need for the recipe, but they are so delicious to have around as a snack that I always make extra. If you can't find snap peas you can substitute Chinese snow peas or even regular shelled sweet peas.

Serving Suggestion

Combines well with Mexican Shrimp and Avocado Salad (page 31) and Grilled Quail with Cherry Salsa (page 39).

Make the soy-glazed almonds.

Preheat the oven to 350°F (175°C). Spread on a cookie sheet:

3 cups (750 ml) whole almonds

Toast the nuts in the oven until they are brown and fragrant.

Mix together in a bowl large enough to hold the nuts:

1 cup (250 ml) soy sauce
1/2 cup (125 ml) sugar
1 Tbsp. (15 ml) chili paste with garlic*

When the nuts come out of the oven, pour them into the soy mixture, toss them to coat thoroughly and let them sit in the mixture for 1/2 hour. Reduce the oven temperature to 300°F (150°C).

Drain the nuts and return them to the baking pan. Put them back in the oven for 15-25 minutes to dry them out. Cool to room temperature. Break the nuts off the cookie sheet and store in an airtight container.

Snap both ends off:

1 lb. (450 g) sugar snap peas

Try to remove the string that runs down the edge of the pea when you snap the ends off. This is quite easy as the ends are connected to the strings.

Have ready:

1 Tbsp. (15 ml) vegetable oil
2 Tbsp. (30 ml) tequila
1/2 cup (125 ml) grapefruit juice
a pinch each salt and pepper
2 grapefruits, peeled and divided into skinless, pithless sections
1/2 cup (125 ml) soy-glazed almonds

Heat a large frying pan. Add the vegetable oil. Heat until the oil is almost smoking. Add the peas and toss them for 20 seconds or so. Add the tequila and toss for 20 seconds. Add the grapefruit juice and the salt and pepper. Put a lid on the pan and steam for 1-2 minutes. Remove the lid and add the grapefruit wedges and almonds. Toss briefly and divide among 4 plates.

*See The Pantry

Mexican Shrimp and Avocado Salad

I developed this recipe for one of our cooking classes. It was an instant hit and we promptly put it on the menu. Florida rock shrimp are small shrimp that are sold peeled and deveined and are very sweet and crunchy when cooked. If you cannot find them, you can substitute spot or tiger prawns, but they must be peeled and deveined after cooking.

Make the dressing.

Combine in a bowl:

2 Tbsp. (30 ml) lime juice
1 Tbsp. (15 ml) red wine vinegar
2 Tbsp. (30 ml) olive oil
1 clove garlic, minced
1 jalapeño chili, minced*
pinch each ground cumin and coriander
salt and pepper to taste

Bring a pot of water to a boil with:

1 tsp. (5 ml) salt

Add:

1/2 lb. (225 g) Florida rock shrimp

Turn off the heat and let the shrimp sit in the water for 1 minute. Drain and put the shrimp into a bowl of cold water to stop the cooking process. Drain.

Combine in a bowl:

1/2 red bell pepper, finely diced
1/4 red onion, finely diced
6 sprigs cilantro, chopped
1 avocado, cut into 1/2" (1-cm) squares

Toss the shrimp and 4 Tbsp. (60 ml) of the dressing with the vegetables.

Divide:

3 cups (750 ml) salad greens

among 4 plates. Drizzle the lettuce with a little of the dressing. Arrange the shrimp and vegetable mixture on top of the salad greens.

Garnish the plates with:

sprigs of cilantro

Serving Suggestion

Combines well with Snap Peas with Grapefruit and Almonds (page 30) and Grilled Quail with Cherry Salsa (page 39).

Asparagus with Mustard Butter

We originally developed this butter for use with Brussels sprouts but the people who didn't like Brussels sprouts were soon asking that we put it on something they did like. We have tried it on asparagus, rapini, several kinds of Chinese greens and cabbage. The tangy flavors of the mustard seem to spark up just about anything.

Prepare the mustard butter.

Combine in a saucepan:
1/4 lb. (115 g) butter
2 Tbsp. (30 ml) Dijon mustard
2 Tbsp. (30 ml) grainy Dijon mustard
1 Tbsp. (15 ml) red mustard seed*
1 Tbsp. (15 ml) yellow mustard seed*
2 Tbsp. (30 ml) lemon juice

Melt them together over a very low heat. Stir the mixture constantly and try not to let it separate. When it looks about the same consistency as mayonnaise, remove from the heat and pour into a container. If the mixture should separate, do not be dismayed. Just take it off the heat and keep stirring until it cools enough to re-emulsify. The mustard butter will keep in the refrigerator for several months.

Snap the woody ends off:
1 lb. (450 g) asparagus

Steam the asparagus until it is crisp-tender. To tell if the asparagus is done, look at the stem end of one of the stalks. If it is not quite done it will have a white dot in the middle of the stalk. When it is done the white spot will have vanished.

Divide the asparagus among 4 plates and spoon 1 Tbsp. (15 ml) of the mustard butter onto each serving. If the butter has been refrigerated, soften it before spooning it onto the asparagus.

*See The Pantry

Serving Suggestion

Combines well with Chrysanthemum Greens with Sesame Dressing (page 19) and Shrimp and Bamboo Happy Cakes (page 21).

Note on Ingredients

Grainy Dijon mustard is sometimes called mieux mustard or country-style Dijon mustard. If you can't find it, just use regular Dijon.

Artichokes with Ginger Vinaigrette

This is a very romantic dish to share with a loved one, pulling the soft leaves from the artichoke and dipping them into the vinaigrette all the way to the tender heart. It is a variation on the classic French dish, Artichokes Vinaigrette. We have given it an Asian flavor by using ginger and Chinese black vinegar.

Bring a large pot of water to a boil.

While the water is heating, remove the stem and the top third of the leaves from:

2 large globe artichokes

Cut in half:

1 lemon

Rub the cut surfaces of the artichokes with the cut surface of one of the lemon halves to stop them from discoloring. Add the lemon halves and the artichokes to the water. Simmer for 1/2 hour or until a skewer can be pushed into the bottom of the artichoke and removed with no resistance.

Meanwhile make the vinaigrette.

Combine in a food processor:

2 tsp. (10 ml) Dijon mustard
2 tsp. (10 ml) grainy Dijon mustard
1/4 cup (60 ml) pickled ginger*
3 Tbsp. (45 ml) Chinese black vinegar*
1 stalk green onion, finely minced
1 clove garlic, finely minced
1 Tbsp. (15 ml) grated fresh ginger
1 Tbsp. (15 ml) sugar
3/4 cup (185 ml) vegetable oil

Process until smooth.

When the artichokes are cooked, remove the center leaves and scrape out the choke (the fine hairlike matter at the bottom of the artichoke) with a spoon. Put the artichokes on a plate and fill the centers with vinaigrette.

*See The Pantry

Serving Suggestion

Combines well with Cioppino Seafood Hotpot (page 36).

Hot and Sour Baby Bok Choy

Vegetables that are commonplace in Asian kitchens are slowly being accepted and used by non-Asians. Bok choy is one of the most familiar of the Chinese greens. Baby bok choy is a miniature version. It has white stalks and green leaves; Shanghai bok choy is the same size, but is completely green. Both are great with this sauce, which is an adaptation of Chinese hot and sour soup.

Make the hot and sour sauce.

Combine in the bowl of a food processor or blender:

10 cloves garlic
2 Tbsp. (30 ml) dried chili flakes
3/4 cup (185 ml) Chinese red vinegar*
3 Tbsp. (45 ml) sugar
1/4 cup (60 ml) mirin*
3 Tbsp. (45 ml) soy sauce

Process for 15-20 seconds. Pour into a pan and boil for 15 minutes. Strain and set aside.

Heat a frying pan until medium hot. Add:

2 bunches baby bok choy
1/2 cup (125 ml) of the sauce.

Toss the bok choy to coat it with the sauce. Cover and steam for 1-2 minutes. Toss again and divide it among 4 plates. If there is a lot of sauce left in the pan, reduce it over high heat until it is syrupy and pour it over the bok choy.

*See The Pantry

Serving Suggestion

Combines well with New Potatoes in Parchment (page 35) and Taro Pancakes with Spicy Tuna (page 38).

New Potatoes in Parchment

Cooking food in parchment paper has the advantage of baking something cut into small pieces without drying it out. The package creates a small steaming environment, so you get wonderful roasted flavor with moist tender vegetables. We also use this method for winter squash.

Serving Suggestion

Combines well with Shrimp and Bamboo Salad (page 13) and Chicken with Prickly Pear Sauce (page 40).

Preheat the oven to 350°F (175°C).

Arrange:

4 sheets of baking parchment, 10" x 10" (25 cm x 25 cm)

on your work surface.

Cut in half:

1 lb. (450 g) new nugget potatoes

Divide the potatoes between the sheets of parchment.

Divide the following between the potatoes:

4 tsp. (20 ml) butter
4 Tbsp. (60 ml) olive oil
4 sprigs fresh thyme
4 whole cloves garlic
a pinch each salt and pepper

Seal the packages by bringing the long edges of the paper together.

Fold the two edges together in small folds down to the level of the potatoes.

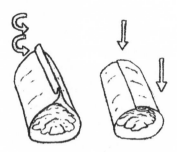

Fold the ends together as if you were wrapping a parcel.

Roll the ends up to seal.

Bake on a baking sheet for 30 minutes.

Note on Ingredients

Nugget potatoes are baby potatoes, and are available throughout the spring and summer. We prefer the red variety for this dish as well as for potato salad. The texture is firm, waxy and not at all mealy or dry. You can substitute regular potatoes cut into 1" (2.5-cm) pieces.

Cioppino Seafood Hotpot

This is our variation on the classic San Francisco seafood soup, cooked in a Japanese-style hotpot and served with a Provençal rouille, a garlicky, red pepper–based sauce. Leftover rouille makes a delicious spread for sandwiches. The flavor depends entirely on the fish stock. You may have access to a place that makes homemade stocks; otherwise, it is well worth the effort to make your own. If you are in a real bind, clam broth is an acceptable substitute for the fish stock.

Make the fish stock.

Combine in a large pot:

1 onion, coarsely chopped
1 stalk of celery, coarsely chopped
2 carrots, coarsely chopped
1 small fennel bulb with the fronds, coarsely chopped
1 large leek, coarsely chopped
4 cloves garlic, coarsely chopped
1/4 cup (60 ml) olive oil

Sauté until slightly softened.

Add:

2 rockfish heads or bones, chopped into 2" (5-cm) pieces and washed
1 Tbsp. (15 ml) fennel seed
1 Tbsp. (15 ml) peppercorns
2 bay leaves
2 quarts (2 l) water

Bring to a simmer and simmer gently for 30 minutes, skimming off the foam that rises to the surface. Strain the stock through a fine mesh strainer into a container. Discard the solids.

Mix 2 cups (500 ml) of the fish stock with:

2 cups (500 ml) Clamato juice
pinch of saffron
1 Tbsp. (15 ml) piri piri sauce

Bring to a boil and cook for 15 minutes. Set aside.

Make the rouille.

Bring to a boil:

2 Tbsp. (30 ml) white wine

Add:

1/4 tsp. (1.2 ml) saffron

Remove from the heat and cool to room temperature. In the bowl of

Note on Ingredients

Piri piri sauce is the national hot sauce of Portugal. You can substitute your favorite hot sauce if you can't find the piri piri. It is available in most Greek or Italian markets.

a food processor, combine the saffron steeped in wine with:

1 cup (250 ml) mayonnaise
1 Tbsp. (15 ml) lemon juice
1 roasted red bell pepper (see page 137)
2 cloves garlic, peeled
1/4 tsp. (1.2 ml) cayenne pepper
salt and pepper to taste

Process until smooth. Set aside.

Assemble the hotpot.

Cut into 1/4" x 3" (.5-cm x 7.5-cm) strips:

1 small red bell pepper
1 small yellow bell pepper
1 small onion
1 small fennel bulb

Sauté the vegetables until soft in:

3 Tbsp. (45 ml) olive oil.

Arrange the vegetables in the bottom of a large Japanese- or Chinese-style hotpot. You can use a regular soup pot, but the presentation will not be as spectacular.

Arrange on top of them:

1 filet of rockfish cut into 8 pieces
12 clams, rinsed
12 mussels, debearded and rinsed
8 small calamari, cleaned and sliced into 1/2" (1-cm) rings
4 pink scallops, rinsed
8 prawns, peeled
a few kale leaves, trimmed of large veins and sliced into ribbons 1/2" (1 cm) wide

Pour enough of the Clamato-fish stock into the hotpot to just cover the vegetables and fish. It should be an inch (2.5 cm) below the lip of the hotpot. Bring it to a boil. Cover and cook for 2 minutes, or until the mussels and clams open up.

Drizzle 1/4 cup (60 ml) of the rouille over the hotpot and serve with fresh crusty bread to sop up the soup.

Serving Suggestion

Combines well with Artichokes with Ginger Vinaigrette (page 33).

Taro Pancakes with Spicy Tuna

These delightful little morsels are a variation on a Hawaiian dish called poke. Our good friends and customers, Alice Macpherson and Doug Bird, came back from a holiday in Hawaii talking about a great taro dish they had while there. That inspired me to create these crisp pancakes with a topping of soft, buttery tuna mixed with chopped peppers and lots of cilantro.

Make the tuna tartare.

Combine in a small bowl:

2 Tbsp. (30 ml) very finely diced red bell pepper

2 Tbsp. (30 ml) very finely diced yellow bell pepper

1 Tbsp. (15 ml) very finely diced jalapeño chili*

4 Tbsp. (60 ml) chopped cilantro leaves

1/4 lb. (115 g) fresh tuna, minced*

1 Tbsp. (15 ml) Thai fish sauce*

1 tsp. (5 ml) lime juice

Make the pancakes.

Combine in a bowl:

2 cups (500 ml) peeled and coarsely grated taro (see Exotic Vegetable Chips, page 29)

1 small onion, grated

1 egg

2 Tbsp. (30 ml) flour

1/2 tsp. (2.5 ml) pepper

1/2 tsp. (2.5 ml) salt

Mix well and form into 2" (5-cm) pancakes about 1/4" (.5 cm) thick. You should have about 18-20 pancakes.

Heat a frying pan and add:

1 Tbsp. (15 ml) butter

1 Tbsp. (15 ml) vegetable oil

When the oil is hot, sauté the pancakes over medium heat for about 2-3 minutes per side. The pancakes should be crisp and golden brown. Arrange them on plates and top with a little mound of the tuna tartare.

*See The Pantry

Serving Suggestion

Combines well with Tea-Smoked Prawn and Shiso Salad (page 14) and Hot and Sour Baby Bok Choy (page 34).

Grilled Quail with Cherry Salsa

Fruit chutneys and salsas are a tradition in many parts of the world. The common ingredient seems to be an acidic fruit, the purpose of the salsa being to spark up the meat that it accompanies. Cherries are not very tart but they have a wonderful rich flavor. Balsamic vinegar provides acidity. This salsa perfectly balances the sweetness of the quail marinade. Cherries are also the first fruit of the year, arriving in late spring to early summer. There is always great excitement in our household when I bring home the first basket of the season. You can substitute Cornish game hens for the quail.

Make the marinade.

Combine in a bowl:

2 cups (500 ml) sweet white dessert wine, preferably muscat

2 cloves garlic, minced

1 onion, chopped

2 bay leaves

3 sprigs fresh thyme

1/2 tsp. (2.5 ml) each salt and pepper

Butterfly

4 whole quail

by cutting them along the backbone with kitchen shears, opening them up and pressing down on the breast bone to flatten them. Add the quail to the marinade and marinate for at least 2 hours.

Make the cherry salsa.

Combine in a bowl:

40 fresh cherries, pitted

2 Tbsp. (30 ml) finely minced red onion

2 Tbsp. (30 ml) balsamic vinegar

4 Tbsp. (60 ml) extra-virgin olive oil

pinch each salt and pepper

6 sprigs cilantro, coarsely chopped

Preheat the barbecue to medium or turn on the oven broiler and adjust the rack to 6" (15 cm) from the heat.

Barbecue the quail skin side down or broil them skin side down on a baking tray. Cook for 4-5 minutes per side. If the skin is beginning to burn, turn them and finish the cooking on the nonpresentation side. Put each quail on a plate and divide the cherry salsa between them.

Serving Suggestion

Combines well with Mexican Shrimp and Avocado Salad (page 31) and Snap Peas with Grapefruit and Almonds (page 30).

Chicken with Prickly Pear Sauce

We refer jokingly to this dish as Custer's last chicken. The olive green of the cactus salsa, the bright red of the prickly pear juice and the brown of the sauce combine with the arrowlike skewers of chicken to paint a very western tableau on the plate. The ingredients in this recipe are a little esoteric, but with a little ingenuity you should be able to put together a dish that looks like the one we make at Raku and tastes great, if not the same as the original. Don't be afraid to substitute!

Make the marinade.

Combine in a saucepan:

1 cup (250 ml) chicken stock
1/2 cup (125 ml) prickly pear juice
1 tsp. (5 ml) dried thyme
1 tsp. (5 ml) dried sage
5 cloves garlic, chopped
4 dried ancho chilis, broken*
2 Tbsp. (30 ml) rice wine vinegar
1 Tbsp. (15 ml) ground coriander
salt and pepper to taste
2 Tbsp. (30 ml) olive oil

Bring the mixture to a boil and cook for 15 minutes. Cool to room temperature.

Prepare the chicken.

Cut into 1" (2.5-cm) cubes:

4 skinless boneless chicken breasts or 6 boneless thighs

Thread the chicken on 8-12 bamboo skewers. Place the skewers in a flat pan with 2/3 of the marinade. Reserve the rest for drizzling on the cooked chicken. Marinate the chicken for half an hour.

Make the cactus salsa.

Combine in a bowl:

3/4 cup (185 ml) cactus paddles, very finely diced
2 Tbsp. (30 ml) green pepper, very finely diced
1 Tbsp. (15 ml) lime juice
1/4 cup (60 ml) pineapple, very finely diced
2 Tbsp. (30 ml) red pepper, very finely diced
2 Tbsp. (30 ml) red onion, minced
1/2 jalapeño chili, seeded and minced*
2 Tbsp. (30 ml) olive oil
salt and pepper to taste

Note on Ingredients

Edible cactus paddles, or *nopales*, are the leaves of an edible cactus plant. You can get prepared, bottled nopales from Mexican groceries or you can buy them fresh. I recommend the bottled kind as the fresh ones can be difficult and potentially painful to work with. If you do use fresh nopales, you must peel the spines and edges of the leaves thoroughly with a vegetable peeler. Always use rubber gloves to handle the leaves, as they have fine, hairlike thorns that are very painful if they contact your skin. Blanch the leaves for a couple of minutes in boiling water and refresh them under cold water before proceeding with the recipe. If you can't find nopales, okra or zucchini make an acceptable substitute. The prickly pear is the fruit of the same cactus that the nopales come from. The juice is not readily available, but may be found in some Mexican groceries. An acceptable substitute is cranberry juice.

Preheat your barbecue grill to medium-high or turn on the oven broiler and adjust the rack to 6" (15 cm) below the heat. Barbecue or broil the skewers on a broiler pan for 3-5 minutes on each side, or until thoroughly cooked.

Arrange the chicken skewers on 4 plates, spoon over a little of the reserved marinade and place a small pile of salsa beside the chicken. If you wish, dot each plate with:

1/2 tsp. (2.5 ml) prickly pear juice

for added color.

*See The Pantry

Serving Suggestion

Combines well with Shrimp and Bamboo Salad (page 13) and New Potatoes in Parchment (page 35).

Summer

The long hot days of summer always take me to the garden for inspiration. It is a season of such abundance—fruits and vegetables flashing by in rapid succession—that it is almost overwhelming. The organic gardening movement has really taken off in recent years and organically grown produce is readily available. We use it at Raku whenever we can—it just tastes better. As in spring, summer flavors should be relatively simple and direct. Salads and barbecue dishes seem natural, as do foods that are simple to prepare and easily enjoyed, like sushi and raw fish dishes. I am particularly influenced by the cuisines of Mexico and the Middle East at this time of year.

Summer

Looking East

It rained last night

but the fat melons

have already forgotten.

—Sodo

Crab and Avocado Hoppa Rolls

Hoppa rolls are salad rolls that combine a meltingly tender coconut crêpe with a mix of lettuce and Thai basil, crabmeat, avocado and a wonderful ginger vinaigrette. We were doing variations on the popular Vietnamese salad roll, but I was not satisfied with the rice wrapper. I was looking through a Sri Lankan cookbook and came across a recipe for bowl-shaped coconut pancakes called "hoppers." These turned my mind to crêpes and I devised this recipe.

Serving Suggestion

These rolls are great with Thai Chicken-Stuffed Chilies (page 55) and Yucca Fritters with Cucumber Raita (page 51). Or, on a hot summer's day, with a glass of beer.

Make the coconut crêpes.

Combine in a large measuring cup:

1 2/3 cups (410 ml) coconut milk (Aroy-d from Thailand is my preferred brand)
5 eggs
2/3 cup (160 ml) flour
1/4 cup (60 ml) rice flour
pinch salt

Whisk until smooth.

Heat a crêpe pan or nonstick skillet until very hot. Rub the surface of the pan with a piece of paper towel that has been dipped in a little vegetable oil.

Pour in enough of the batter to coat the bottom of the pan thinly.

Let the surface of the crêpe dry out a little, moving the pan around the burner to dry any very wet spots. This will take about 20 seconds. Loosen the top edge of the crêpe from the pan with cooking chopsticks or the handle of a wooden spoon.

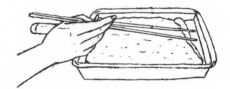

Put the chopsticks or spoon handle across the top of the pan and flip the top edge of the crêpe up onto it. Gently pull the crêpe towards you, lifting it off the pan.

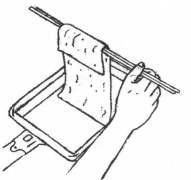

When it is completely off the pan lay the bottom edge of the crêpe at the top of the pan and put it back into the pan with the uncooked side down.

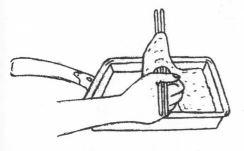

Let the crêpe dry for about 5 seconds and then turn it onto a plate. It should only take a couple of minutes for each crêpe. This recipe makes about 8-10 crêpes; stack them on a plate and set them aside until you are ready to assemble the rolls. The crêpes will not stick together.

Make the ginger vinaigrette (see recipe page 33).

Have ready the crepes, the ginger vinaigrette and:
30 Thai basil leaves*
3 cups (750 ml) mixed lettuce, washed and torn into small pieces
1/2 lb. (225 g) cooked crabmeat
2 avocados, seeded, peeled and cut into 9 slices each

Lay 6 crepes out flat on the counter.

Place 5 Thai basil leaves in a line across the bottom of each crêpe. On top of these place 1/2 cup (125 ml) of the lettuce. Spoon 2 Tbsp. (30 ml) of the vinaigrette across the lettuce. Sprinkle 1/6 of the crab over the lettuce and top with 3 of the avocado slices.

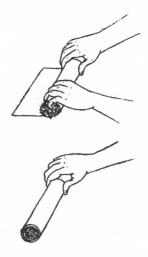

Starting at the bottom edge of each crêpe, roll it around the other ingredients, leaving the ends of the roll open. Cut each roll into 4 pieces, arrange them on salad plates and serve.

*See The Pantry

Barbecue Pork and Papaya Rolls

We like to do variations on salad rolls during the summer. I find the traditional Vietnamese shrimp rolls a little bland, so I devised a few new ways to spark them up. It is important to use soft lettuce leaves for these rolls, as the crisper varieties will rip the rice wrappers. If you prefer, use blanched prawns instead of pork.

Make the Vietnamese salad dressing (see page 16).

Bring a small pot of water to a boil. Add:

1 small package of bean thread noodles*

Cook for 1 minute. Drain and rinse with cold water.

Set out:
4 Vietnamese rice wrappers
1/2 cup (125 ml) Thai basil leaves*
4 stalks green onion
1 cup (250 ml) mixed lettuce
1/2 lb. (225 g) Chinese-style barbecued pork, shredded
1/2 papaya, sliced lengthwise into 8 pieces

Reconstitute the rice wrappers by dipping them in a bowl of hot water and laying them on the counter. They will soften after a couple of minutes. If there are any hard parts left, rub them with a little more water.

Place the basil leaves in a line across the bottom third of the wrappers, dividing them equally among the 4 wrappers. Lay a green onion stalk across the basil leaves. Arrange 1/4 cup (60 ml) of lettuce on each of the wrappers. Put some of the noodles on top of the lettuce and top with the shredded pork and papaya. Fold the bottom edge of the wrapper up over the filling. Holding the bottom edge in place, fold each of the sides in to close off the ends of the roll, then finish rolling towards the top until everything is completely enclosed.

Serve with Vietnamese salad dressing as a dipping sauce.

*See The Pantry

Note on Ingredients

As you walk down the street of just about any Chinese market anywhere in North America you can't help but notice the whole roast pigs and glistening chunks of succulent **barbecued pork** hanging in the windows of most butcher shops. These items, along with **barbecued duck,** are among the true treasures of any Chinatown. Don't be shy: just go in, point at what you want and ask for a pound or two. You won't be disappointed.

Vietnamese rice wrappers are very thin, round wrappers made from rice flour and water. They are sold in their dry form and look somewhat like thin plastic disks. You can find them in most Asian markets. If you need a substitute, try making the coconut crêpes on page 46.

Serving Suggestion

Combines well with Yucatan Salmon with Tomatillo Sauce (page 69) and Yaki Onigiri (page 141).

Thai Tuna Carpaccio

Tuna carpaccio is one of the first dishes I ever created. I have long been a fan of beef carpaccio and thought that tuna would be an admirable stand-in. To give the fish a slightly charred flavor, we sear it on one side before slicing and dressing it with a dynamite, Vietnamese-influenced dressing.

Make the dressing.

Combine in a food processor or mortar:
1 jalapeño chili, minced*
1 clove garlic, minced
2 Tbsp. (30 ml) sugar

Process or grind with a pestle until the mixture is relatively smooth and liquid.

Add:
1/2 cup (125 ml) Thai fish sauce*
juice of 1 lime
zest and juice of 1 kaffir lime*

Stir to combine.

Preheat the barbecue to medium or heat a nonstick frying pan until it is hot enough to make a drop of water sizzle on contact. Lay on the grill or in the pan:
4 1/4-lb. (115-g) pieces of tuna

Sear the tuna on one side; you want to have the bottom just cooked and the rest of the tuna raw. This will not take long.

Remove the tuna from the heat and set it on a cutting board. Slice it into as many very thin slices as you can.

Divide the tuna among 4 plates, laying it out in an attractive pattern. Drizzle 2 Tbsp. (30 ml) of the dressing over each serving of tuna. You can garnish it with:
Japanese pickled ginger*
sprigs of Thai basil*

*See The Pantry

Serving Suggestion

Combines well with Corn Cakes with Jalapeño Créma (page 59) and Berebere Ethiopian Chicken (page 70).

Note on Equipment

Lemon zesters are one of the handiest and most versatile tools in the kitchen. Laurie uses hers not only to zest, but also to whisk eggs, pry lids off tins and as a makeshift measuring spoon. Finding a good one can be very tricky, though. Price or brand name is no real indicator of quality. It is almost worth taking a lemon into the store to test them out! When you find one that works, cherish it.

Snap Peas with Soy and Sake

This recipe is so fast and easy that it is hard to believe it could be so good. There is something Zen-like in the simple pure flavors. You can substitute snow peas or regular shelled peas if you can't get snap peas.

Snap the ends and pull the strings off:

1 lb. (450 g) of snap peas

Heat a sauté pan over high heat until medium-hot.

Add:

1 tsp. (5 ml) vegetable oil

Heat for 15 seconds. Add the peas. Stir-fry for 1 minute. Add:

1/4 cup (60 ml) sake

Reduce the heat. Stir, then cover the pan and steam for a minute. Add:

1 Tbsp. (15 ml) soy sauce

Remove the lid and stir and cook the peas until most of the liquid is gone. Divide the peas among 4 plates and sprinkle with:

sancho pepper*

*See The Pantry

Serving Suggestion

Combines well with Green Onion Cakes with Lemon Dipping Sauce (page 52) and Soft-Shell Crab with Pirates Chili Sauce (page 54).

Crab and Avocado Hoppa
Rolls, page 46

Chinese-Style Leeks
Mimosa, page 74

Yucca Fritters with Cucumber Raita

People love potato pancakes and I love to experiment with unusual vegetables! Yucca, or cassava, is grown in many areas of the world, including the Caribbean. These fritters are more like latkes and have a little bite of curry which is offset by the soothing flavor of the cucumber raita. If you can't find yucca, substitute potatoes.

Make the cucumber raita.

Quarter and thinly slice:
1 small English cucumber

Put it into a strainer and sprinkle with:
1 tsp. (5 ml) salt

Let it drain for 20 minutes over the sink. Rinse with a little water and then pat the slices dry with a towel.

Combine the cucumbers in a bowl with:
1/2 cup (125 ml) plain yoghurt
1/4 tsp. (1.2 ml) ground cumin
1/4 tsp. (1.2 ml) ground coriander
1/4 tsp. (1.2 ml) sugar
1/2 tsp. (2.5 ml) red mustard seeds*

Set aside.

Make the fritters.

Combine in a bowl:
2 cups (500 ml) coarsely grated yucca
1 small onion, grated
1 egg
2 Tbsp. (30 ml) flour
1/2 tsp. (2.5 ml) pepper
1/2 tsp. (2.5 ml) salt
1 Tbsp. (15 ml) mild curry paste or powder

Mix well and form the mixture into 2" (5-cm) pancakes about 1/4" (.5 cm) thick.

Heat a frying pan and add:
1 Tbsp. (15 ml) butter
1 Tbsp. (15 ml) vegetable oil

When the oil is hot, add the fritters and sauté over medium heat for about 2-3 minutes per side. The fritters should be crisp and golden brown.

Arrange the fritters on 4 plates and top with a little mound of the raita.

*See The Pantry

Serving Suggestion

Combines well with Barbecue Pork and Papaya Rolls (page 48) and Yaki Onigiri (page 141).

Green Onion Cakes with Lemon Dipping Sauce

I always enjoyed green onion cakes at Chinese restaurants but found them a little greasy. We thought grilling would cut down on the oil and give them a nice flavor. These cakes have seen a multitude of dipping sauces in their time at Raku; this lemon one is the latest.

Prepare the lemon dipping sauce.

Combine in a bowl:
1 cup (250 ml) hoisin sauce*
zest of 2 lemons
1/4 cup (60 ml) lemon juice

Make the onion cakes.

Combine in the bowl of a mixer fitted with a dough hook:
2 1/2 cups (625 ml) all-purpose flour
1/2 cup (125 ml) wheat starch

With the machine running, add:
1 cup (250 ml) hot water

Process the mixture until it forms a ball. If it is sticky, add more flour. Turn the ball out onto a floured surface and knead by hand for a minute to develop the gluten. Let the dough rest for about 15 minutes.

Combine in a bowl:
1 1/2 cups (375 ml) thinly sliced green onions
1/2 cup (125 ml) coarsely chopped coriander leaves
1/2 cup (125 ml) finely chopped garlic chives

Set out:
3 Tbsp. (45 ml) sesame oil
1/4 cup (60 ml) sesame seeds
1 1/2 Tbsp. (22 ml) salt

Roll the dough out into a log shape about a foot (30 cm) long and cut it into 8 pieces. Form each piece into a ball. With a rolling pin flatten each ball into a 7" (18-cm) round. Lay the rounds out on your work surface.

Brush each of the rounds with the sesame oil, sprinkle with sesame seeds and salt, then divide the green onion mixture among them. Roll the dough up like a jelly roll and press down the ends of the roll to seal them.

Take one end of the roll and wind it around the other to end up with a coil. Tuck the loose end under and flatten the coil slightly with the palm of your hand. With a rolling pin, flatten the coils into

Note on Ingredients

Wheat starch is exactly that, the starch component of wheat flour. It is used for making many types of Chinese dumplings and can be found in all Chinese groceries. It is also available in health food stores.

7" (18-cm) circles. The green onions may pop out here and there, but don't worry, just continue to gently roll them.

At this point you can immediately cook the cakes or you can pile them up, separated by plastic wrap, and freeze them. They are great to pull out of the freezer and fire onto the grill or into a pan for a quick snack.

To cook them, preheat your barbecue grill to medium heat. Brush the cakes with a little oil and lay them on the grill. When the top surface looks a little translucent and the edges are looking white, about 4 minutes, turn the cakes over and cook for 2 more minutes. Remove from the grill and cut into wedges. Serve with the lemon dipping sauce.

*See The Pantry

Serving Suggestion

Combines well with Snap Peas with Soy and Sake (page 50) and Soft-Shell Crab with Pirates Chili Sauce (page 54).

Soft-Shell Crab with Pirates Chili Sauce

Soft-shell crabs are only available fresh for a very short time in the summer and realistically only on the east coast where they are harvested. Luckily they are available frozen, not quite as good as the fresh, but still very tasty. I sometimes buy a jar of commercially prepared pirates chili sauce called sambal badjak and use it in place of the reconstituted dried chilies in this recipe. The bottled sauce has lost a lot of subtle nuances of flavor, but if you beef it up with the other ingredients, the resulting sauce is very good.

Serving Suggestion

Combines well with Green Onion Cakes with Lemon Dipping Sauce (page 52) and Snap Peas with Soy and Sake (page 50).

Make the pirates chili sauce.

Combine:

1 cup (250 ml) dried red chilies
1 cup (250 ml) of water

Soak the chilies for one hour, then place them and the soaking water in a food processor with:

1/2 small onion, sliced
3 cloves garlic, sliced
1 Tbsp. (15 ml) shrimp paste*
1 tsp. (5 ml) salt
1 Tbsp. (15 ml) sugar
2 Tbsp. (30 ml) tamarind purée or concentrate*

Purée the mixture.

In a saucepan, melt:

3 Tbsp. (45 ml) butter

Add the chili sauce and:

1 bay leaf

Cook over low heat for 10-15 minutes, or until most of the liquid has evaporated.

Prepare the crabs.

Rinse and pat dry:

4 large soft-shell crabs

Dredge the crabs in:

1 cup (250 ml) rice flour

Shred:

1/4 head napa cabbage or sui choy

Toss it with:

4 Tbsp. (60 ml) soy lime dressing (see page 135)

Heat a sauté pan and add:

4 Tbsp. (60 ml) vegetable oil
2 Tbsp. (30 ml) butter

Add the crabs and sauté until brown and crisp on both sides. Remove the crabs and drain them on paper towel for a few seconds.

Divide the cabbage mixture among 4 plates, cut the crabs in half and arrange them so it looks like they are climbing the pile of cabbage. Spoon a line of pirates chili sauce across the top of each crab.

Thai Chicken-Stuffed Chilies

This recipe is a variation on Mexican Chilies Rellenos. I wanted to eliminate the deep-frying and show the rich contrast of colors between the red and green Anaheim chilies. If you can't find red Anaheims, just use the green.

Serving Suggestion

Combines well with Crab and Avocado Hoppa Rolls (page 46) and Yucca Fritters with Cucumber Raita (page 51).

Heat your barbecue to medium or turn on the oven broiler and adjust the rack to 6" (15 cm) below the heat.

Lay out:

4 green Anaheim chilies*
4 red Anaheim chilies*
4 sprigs Thai basil*

Rub the peppers with a little oil and grill or broil them, turning them, until the skin on each side is black and blistered. Remove from the heat and place in a plastic bag to cool for 15 minutes. Remove them from the bag and peel off the skin. Make a slit down one side of each pepper and open to expose the seeds. Snip the seed ball near the stem with a pair of kitchen scissors and pull out the seeds. Dip the peppers in a bowl of water to remove any seeds that remain. Pat dry.

Heat a sauté pan over high heat. Add:

3 Tbsp. (45 ml) vegetable oil
5 cloves garlic, minced
2 jalapeño chilies, minced, seeds left in*

Sauté for a minute. Add:

1 lb. (450 g) ground chicken

Sauté until the chicken is completely cooked. Add:

3 Tbsp. (45 ml) Thai fish sauce*
2 Tbsp. (30 ml) soy sauce
1/4 cup (60 ml) water
2 Tbsp. (30 ml) sugar
4 Thai bird chilies, minced* **(optional)**

Cook, stirring until the liquid is almost all absorbed.

Set out 4 plates. Divide the chicken mixture among the plates, arranging it in 2 rows about the length of the chilies. Place 4 Thai basil leaves on each row of chicken. Lay one green pepper on top of one pile and one red on the other. Tuck the edges of the chilies under the chicken to make them look like whole chilies again. You can reheat them in the microwave if they have become too cool during the assembly.

*See The Pantry

Summer

Looking West

Quiet morning:

steam rises

from the awakening garden.

Tuna and Olive Terrine

Tuna and black olives are two quintessential Mediterranean foodstuffs. When combined with a Japanese esthetic and preparation they become something quite different—the flavors are bright, clear and hauntingly familiar, but when presented in this way they also challenge your expectations. The tapenade from this recipe is a wonderful thing to have in the fridge. It is a black olive and caper purée that is used as a dip, spread or base for pasta sauce in the south of France. At my house it goes into all sorts of sandwiches and onto pizzas and pastas.

Make the black olive tapenade.

Combine in the bowl of a food processor:

2 cups (500 ml) ripe Italian-style black olives, pitted
2 cloves garlic
4 anchovy fillets or 3 tsp. (45 ml) anchovy paste
2 Tbsp. (30 ml) capers
zest of 1 small orange
1/2 cup (125 ml) extra-virgin olive oil
1 tsp. (5 ml) brandy

Process until smooth.

Set out:

4 pieces sashimi-grade tuna, about 3" x 1 1/2" x 1 1/2" (7.5 cm x 3.75 cm x 3.75 cm) in size*
32 Thai basil leaves*

Cut each of the pieces of tuna into 8 slices. Place 2 slices of tuna on each serving plate. Spread a thin layer of the black olive tapenade on the slices. Lay a basil leaf on top of the tapenade and then lay another slice of tuna on top of that. Repeat the process until you have 2 piles, 4 slices high, on each plate. You should have a perfect basil leaf on the top of each pile.

*See The Pantry

Serving Suggestion

Combines well with Endive Wrapped in Pancetta (page 64) and Salmon with Purple Basil Vinaigrette (page 68).

Corn Cakes with Jalapeño Créma

This is the runaway favorite of the many different pancakes we serve at Raku. The sweetness of corn mingled with the subtle richness of coconut milk in this recipe make it a winner. Use fresh corn in season to make this dish really shine, but canned corn is an acceptable substitute if you have a craving in the middle of winter.

Make the jalapeño créma.

Combine in a small bowl:
1/2 cup (125 ml) sour cream
1/4 jalapeño chili, minced*
pinch salt

Make the pancake mixture.

Combine in a bowl:
3/4 cup (185 ml) all-purpose flour
1/2 tsp. (2.5 ml) baking powder
1/2 tsp. (2.5 ml) salt
1/2 tsp. (2.5 ml) Szechuan peppercorns, toasted and ground*

Make a well in the center of the flour mixture. Add:
1 egg
1/4 cup (60 ml) coconut milk
1 tsp. (5 ml) grated fresh ginger
1/2 tsp. (2.5 ml) Vietnamese chili sauce with garlic*
1 1/2 cups (375 ml) fresh corn kernels
12 sprigs cilantro leaves, chopped
1/4 cup (60 ml) minced green onion

Stir lightly to combine. Do not overmix or the pancakes will be tough.

Heat in a frying pan:
1 Tbsp. (15 ml) butter
2 Tbsp. (30 ml) vegetable oil

When the butter starts to foam, add the batter in heaping tablespoons to make as many pancakes as will comfortably fit into the pan, allowing little space between them. Lower the heat so the pancakes don't burn. After 1-2 minutes flip the pancakes and cook for another minute or two, or until the pancakes are crisp and golden. Keep the cooked pancakes warm in a low oven until you are finished cooking all of the batter.

Arrange them on 4 plates and garnish with a little dab of the jalapeño créma.

Serving Suggestion
Combines well with Thai Tuna Carpaccio (page 49) and Berebere Ethiopian Chicken (page 70).

Smoked Duck Roll

A variation on our hoppa roll, using hot-smoked duck breast and cranberry ginger sauce instead of crab and pickled ginger vinaigrette. Not surprisingly, it was Thanksgiving weekend that inspired this variation. You should be able to find smoked duck at specialty poultry shops. If you like, try substituting smoked turkey or ham for the duck. For some visual help with the crêpes, see the illustrations for Crab and Avocado Hoppa Rolls (page 46).

Make the onion crêpes.

Combine in a large measuring cup:

1 1/2 cups (375 ml) cereal cream
5 eggs
2/3 cup (160 ml) flour
1/4 cup (60 ml) rice flour
pinch salt
1 tsp. (5 ml) coarse black pepper
2 green onions, finely chopped

Whisk until smooth.

Heat a crêpe pan or nonstick skillet until very hot. Rub the surface of the pan with a piece of paper towel that has been dipped in a little vegetable oil. Pour in enough of the batter to coat the bottom of the pan thinly. Let the surface of the crêpe dry out a little, moving the pan around the burner to dry any very wet spots. This will take about 20 seconds.

Loosen the top edge of the crêpe from the pan with cooking chopsticks or the handle of a wooden spoon. Put the chopsticks or spoon handle across the top of the pan and flip the top edge of the crêpe up onto it. Gently pull the crêpe towards you, lifting it off the pan.

Lay the bottom edge of the crêpe at the top of the pan and put it back into the pan with the uncooked side down. Let the crêpe dry for about 5 seconds and then slide it onto a plate. It should only take a couple of minutes for each crêpe. This recipe makes about 8-10 crêpes; stack them on a plate and set them aside until you are ready to assemble the rolls. The crêpes will not stick together.

Make the cranberry sauce.

Combine in a small saucepan:

1/2 cup (125 ml) cranberries
1/2 cup (125 ml) orange juice
1/4 cup (60 ml) sugar
1 Tbsp. (15 ml) fresh grated ginger

Cook the mixture until the berries lose their shape, about 10 minutes.

Process until smooth in the bowl of a food processor or blender.

Set aside.

Prepare the rolls.

Have ready the crêpes, the cranberry sauce and:

1/2 lb. (225 g) smoked duck breast, fat peeled off, cut into long, narrow strips
8 stalks green onion
4 cups (1 l) mixed lettuce, torn into small pieces

Lay 8 crêpes out flat on the counter. Place 1/2 cup (125 ml) of the lettuce across the bottom of each crêpe. Spoon 2 Tbsp. (30 ml) of the sauce across the lettuce, then sprinkle 1/8 of the duck over the lettuce and top with an onion strip. Starting at the bottom edge of each crêpe, roll the crêpe around the other ingredients, leaving the ends open. Cut each roll into 4 pieces and arrange on salad plates.

Serving Suggestion

Combines well with Jamaican Jerk Prawns (page 66) and Yaki Onigiri (page 141).

B.C. Indian Candy Roll

This is another variation on the hoppa-roll theme. This one features all British Columbia products, including Indian candy, which is the sweet-cured, heavily smoked belly pieces of the salmon. They are quite chewy and are sometimes referred to as salmon jerky. For a little visual help with the crêpes in this recipe, see the illustrations for Crab and Avocado Hoppa Rolls (page 46).

Make the buckwheat crêpes.

Combine in a large measuring cup:

1 1/2 cups (375 ml) cereal cream
5 eggs
2/3 cup (160 ml) flour
1/4 cup (60 ml) rice flour
pinch salt

Whisk until smooth.

Heat a crêpe pan or nonstick skillet until very hot. Rub the surface of the pan with a piece of paper towel that has been dipped in a little vegetable oil.

Pour in enough of the batter to coat the bottom of the pan thinly. Let the surface of the crêpe dry a little, moving the pan around the burner to dry any very wet spots. This will take about 20 seconds.

Loosen the top edge of the crêpe from the pan with cooking chopsticks or the handle of a wooden spoon. Put the chopsticks or spoon handle across the top of the pan and flip the top edge of the crêpe up onto it. Gently pull the crêpe towards you, lifting it off the pan.

Lay the bottom edge of the crêpe at the top of the pan and put it back into the pan with the uncooked side down. Let the crêpe dry for about 5 seconds and then slide it onto a plate. It should only take a couple of minutes for each crêpe. This recipe makes about 8-10 crêpes; stack them on a plate and set them aside until you are ready to assemble the rolls. The crêpes will not stick together.

Prepare the rolls.

Have ready:

4 cups (1 l) mixed lettuce, washed and torn into small pieces
1/3 cup (80 ml) creamed hot horseradish sauce
1/2 lb. (225 g) Indian candy (or hot-smoked salmon)
8 pieces green onion

Lay 8 crêpes out flat on the counter. Place 1/2 cup (125 ml) of the lettuce across the bottom of each crêpe. Spoon 2 tsp. (10 ml) of the sauce across the lettuce, then sprinkle 1/8 of the Indian candy over the lettuce and top with an onion strip. Starting at the bottom edge of each crêpe, roll the crêpe around the other ingredients, leaving the ends of the roll open. Cut each roll into 4 pieces, arrange them on salad plates and serve.

Serving Suggestion

Combines well with Spicy Calamari with Lime (page 65) and Yaki Onigiri (page141).

Endive Wrapped in Pancetta

The Japanese are fond of wrapping things in bacon before grilling them. We started wrapping vegetables in pancetta—Italian cured, unsmoked bacon—which is available in most Italian groceries and in the deli section in many supermarkets. It has less fat and a more complex flavor than regular bacon. It should be thinly sliced but still intact. You can substitute blanched green beans, asparagus or even oysters for the endive.

Make a vinaigrette.

Combine in a small bowl:

2 Tbsp. (30 ml) balsamic vinegar

4 Tbsp. (60 ml) extra-virgin olive oil

1/4 tsp. (1.2 ml) salt

1/4 tsp. (1.2 ml) pepper

Set aside.

Lay out:

8 thin but intact slices of pancetta

4 heads Belgian endive, cut in half

Place the endive halves on the pancetta slices and roll the pancetta around the endive. Secure with a couple of toothpicks.

Preheat the barbecue to medium or turn on the oven broiler and adjust the rack to 6" (15 cm) below the heat. Grill or broil the wrapped endive for 3-4 minutes per side. Remove to 4 plates and drizzle with a little of the vinaigrette.

Serving Suggestion

Combines well with Tuna and Olive Terrine (page 58) and Salmon with Purple Basil Vinaigrette (page 68).

Spicy Calamari with Lime

In Japan calamari are prepared in countless ways, from velvety, toothsome sashimi to aromatic dried squid snacks. Calamari also come in all sizes. The preferred size for grilling in Japan is about 10" (25 cm) long, not including the tentacles. These grill up quite firm, almost rubbery some would say! We prefer the small California squid for most of our dishes. They are only 3-6" (7.5-15 cm) long. If you do not overcook them they are always tender.

Serving Suggestion

Combines well with B.C. Indian Candy Roll (page 62) and Yaki Onigiri (page 141).

Make the marinade.

Combine in a large bowl:
1/3 cup (80 ml) mirin*
2 Tbsp. (30 ml) soy sauce
2 tsp. (10 ml) Vietnamese chili sauce with garlic*
1/4 tsp. (1.2 ml) cayenne pepper
1/4 tsp. (1.2 ml) ground cinnamon
1/4 tsp. (1.2 ml) ground cloves
1/4 tsp. (1.2 ml) ground white pepper
1/4 tsp. (1.2 ml) ground star anise (or ground anise seeds)

Clean:
2 lbs. (900 g) small California squid (see page 12 for cleaning instructions)

Marinate the calamari for 1-2 hours.

Make the mustard green slaw.

Combine in a bowl:
1/2 carrot, grated
1/4 very small head red cabbage, grated
1 large bunch mustard greens, sliced into very thin chiffonade

Combine in a small saucepan:
2 Tbsp. (30 ml) pickling spice
1/4 cup (60 ml) apple cider vinegar
3/4 cup (185 ml) rice wine vinegar
1 Tbsp. (15 ml) salt
1 Tbsp. (15 ml) sugar

Bring the mixture to a boil, then strain it onto the mustard green mixture. Toss the vegetables with the vinegars and set aside to marinate until the squid is ready.

Preheat the barbecue or turn on the oven broiler and adjust the rack to 4" (10 cm) below the heat. Place the calamari on the grill. By the time you have finished putting the last piece on, the first piece will be ready to turn over. Turn them all over, then start taking them off. Total cooking time should be about 2-3 minutes. Quickly slice the tubes into rings and pile onto 4 plates.

Cut:
1 lime
into quarters and squeeze one piece onto each pile of calamari. Garnish with a small handful of the slaw and sprinkle with a few:
sesame seeds

Jamaican Jerk Prawns

Habañero chilies—the hottest in the world—are available in all Mexican groceries and in many supermarkets. If you can't find them, substitute double the quantity of jalapeños; the flavor will be quite different but no less tasty. This marinade is great for pork, chicken and the prawns discussed here. It is predictably Very, Very Spicy!

Prepare the marinade.

Combine in the bowl of a food processor:

5 habañero peppers, fresh or pickled
2 Tbsp. (30 ml) ground rosemary
2 Tbsp. (30 ml) parsley
2 Tbsp. (30 ml) dried basil
2 Tbsp. (30 ml) dried thyme
2 Tbsp. (30 ml) mustard seed
4 green onions
1 tsp. (5 ml) salt
1 tsp. (5 ml) pepper
1/4 cup (60 ml) lemon juice
1/4 cup (60 ml) Dijon mustard
2 Tbsp. (30 ml) orange juice
2 Tbsp. (30 ml) white wine vinegar

Process until smooth.

Thread:

24 medium prawns

onto bamboo skewers, 3 per skewer. It is up to you whether or not you want to leave the shells on. Prawns cooked in their shells have a much richer flavor and don't dry out as much as ones cooked with the shells removed. Put the skewered prawns into a flat dish and cover them with 3/4 of the marinade. Reserve the remaining marinade. Marinate for 1/2 hour.

Preheat your barbecue grill or oven broiler and adjust the rack to 6" (15 cm) below the heat. Barbecue or broil the skewers for 2-3 minutes on each side, or until just done. Try not to overcook the prawns or they will be tough and will lose a lot of flavor. Serve them with the reserved marinade as a dip.

Serving Suggestion

Combines well with Smoked Duck Roll (page 60) and Yaki Onigiri (page 141).

Grilled Jumbo Prawns with Thai Basil Vinaigrette

Try this vinaigrette with grilled salmon or as the dressing for an Asian-flavored Salade Nicoise.

Make the Thai basil vinaigrette.

Combine in the bowl of a food processor or blender:

8 sprigs Thai basil, leaves only*
1 whole jalapeño chili*
2 Tbsp. (30 ml) rice wine vinegar
6 Tbsp. (90 ml) vegetable oil
1 clove garlic
1 Tbsp. (15 ml) lime juice
1 Tbsp. (15 ml) Thai fish sauce*
1/2 tsp. (2.5 ml) sugar

Process until smooth. Set aside.

Peel and devein:

12 jumbo tiger prawns

Thread the prawns, 3 to a skewer, on 4 bamboo skewers.

If you wish, weave:

2 pandan leaves
between the prawns while skewering.

Heat your barbecue grill to hot or turn on the broiler and adjust the oven rack to 6" (15 cm) beneath the heat. Grill or broil the prawns for 2 minutes on each side, or until they are done to your liking.

Spoon some of the vinaigrette onto the serving plates and lay the prawns on top of it.

Garnish with:

4 sprigs Thai basil*

*See The Pantry

Serving Suggestion

Combines well with Snap Peas with Soy and Sake (page 50) and Corn Cakes with Jalapeño Créma (page 59).

Note on Ingredients

Pandan leaves are the leaves of the screwpine plant native to Southeast Asia. They are not eaten but are used to wrap foods and impart a wonderful fragrance. They can be found at Asian markets that carry Thai food.

Salmon with Purple Basil Vinaigrette

Salmon is the one food item that immediately comes up when people talk about British Columbia. For that reason we have plenty of recipes using it. The vinaigrette in this dish calls for the very fragrant but rare purple basil. You may be able to find it in specialty produce markets or you could try growing it yourself. The seeds are quite readily available. You can substitute regular or Thai basil for a nice but quite different dish.

Make the vinaigrette.

Combine in the bowl of a food processor or blender:

8 sprigs purple basil, leaves only
1 Tbsp. (15 ml) rice wine vinegar
4 Tbsp. (60 ml) vegetable oil
1 clove garlic
1 Tbsp. (15 ml) lime juice
1 Tbsp. (15 ml) Thai fish sauce*
1/2 tsp. (2.5 ml) sugar
salt to taste

Process until smooth. Set aside.

Set out:

4 6-oz. (180-g) filet pieces of salmon

Preheat your barbecue grill to medium-high or turn on the oven broiler and adjust the rack to 6" (15 cm) below the heat. Grill or broil the fish for 2-3 minutes on each side, or until it is done to your liking. Pool some vinaigrette on each plate and place the salmon on top of the sauce. Garnish with a sprig of purple basil.

*See The Pantry

Serving Suggestion

Combines well with Tuna and Olive Terrine (page 58) and Endive Wrapped in Pancetta (page 64).

Yucatan Salmon with Tomatillo Sauce

I love the idea of spreading a piece of meat or fish with a savory paste before grilling. The result is highly flavored, with a crisp crust of spices. Tomatillos, which look like green tomatoes with a husk, give a bright sharp taste to this sauce, making it a perfect foil for the rich, spicy salmon. They are available in Mexican groceries and in many supermarkets. You can substitute green tomatoes, or red ones for a slight variation.

Make the chili paste.

Combine in a bowl:

1/2 cup (125 ml) chili powder
1 Tbsp. (15 ml) ground cumin
1 Tbsp. (15 ml) ground coriander
1 clove garlic, grated
1/4 tsp. (1.2 ml) ground cloves
1/4 tsp. (1.2 ml) ground allspice
1/2 tsp. (2.5 ml) ground anise seed
1/4 cup (60 ml) olive oil

Set aside. This will keep in the refrigerator for weeks.

Make the tomatillo sauce.

Combine in the bowl of a food processor or blender:

9 medium tomatillos, grilled or broiled until soft and brown on the outside
1 clove garlic
1 small bunch cilantro
1/4 tsp. (1.2 ml) salt
2 Tbsp. (30 ml) rice wine vinegar
1/4 cup (60 ml) olive oil

Process until almost smooth, but still a little chunky.

Set out:

4 6-oz. (180-g) filet pieces of salmon

Preheat your barbecue grill to medium-high or turn on the oven broiler and adjust the rack to 6" (15 cm) below the heat. Grill or broil the fish for 2-3 minutes on one side. Spread the uncooked side with the chili paste and grill this side for another 2-3 minutes, or until the fish is done to your liking. Pool some tomatillo sauce on each plate and place the salmon on top. Garnish with a sprig of cilantro or a husk from the tomatillos.

Serving Suggestion

Combines well with Barbecue Pork and Papaya Rolls (page 48) and Yaki Onigiri (page 141).

Berebere Ethiopian Chicken

Berebere sauce is sometimes called the ketchup of Ethiopia. It is used as a marinade, dipping sauce and condiment in a large variety of dishes. The recipe uses red wine as one of the ingredients, acknowledging the French influence on the region. You can make this as spicy as you want, but don't overpower the interesting mélange of flavors from the other spices.

Make the berebere paste.

Combine in a sauté pan:

1 tsp. (5 ml) powdered ginger
1 tsp. (5 ml) red pepper flakes
1 tsp. (5 ml) ground cardamom
2 tsp. (10 ml) ground coriander
1 tsp. (5 ml) star anise, crushed
1 tsp. (5 ml) ground turmeric
1 tsp. (5 ml) dry mustard
1 tsp. (5 ml) ground fenugreek
1 tsp. (5 ml) grated nutmeg
1 tsp. (5 ml) ground cinnamon
1 tsp. (5 ml) ground allspice
1 tsp. (5 ml) ground black pepper
2 tsp. (10 ml) salt
2 Tbsp. (30 ml) cayenne
1/2 cup (125 ml) paprika

Dry-roast the spices in the pan over low heat for 3-4 minutes. Stir constantly to avoid scorching. The mixture will be very aromatic! Add:

1/2 cup (125 ml) vegetable oil
and mix thoroughly. Add:
1 cup (250 ml) red wine
1/2 cup (125 ml) orange juice
1/4 cup (60 ml) honey

Cook for 5 minutes, stirring all the while. The mixture will be very thick. Remove to a container. This paste will keep indefinitely in the refrigerator.

Cut into 1" (2.5-cm) cubes:
4 skinless, boneless chicken breasts or 6 thighs

Thread the chicken onto 8-12 bamboo skewers. Coat the skewered chicken with some of the berebere paste. Cover and refrigerate for at least 30 minutes. Reserve the remaining paste for another use.

Preheat your barbecue to medium-high or turn on the oven broiler and adjust the rack to 6" (15 cm) below the heat. Barbecue or broil the skewers for 3-5 minutes on each side, or until thoroughly cooked. Watch it carefully because the paste is slightly sweet and burns easily.

Serving Suggestion

Combines well with Thai Tuna Carpaccio (page 49) and Corn Cakes with Jalapeño Créma (page 59).

Autumn

Autumn always brings the sight and scent of falling leaves and the promise of wild mushrooms and game. Wild mushrooms were a treasure I was finally able to explore when we went to Japan. Most of the varieties that are available in Japan are cultivated, but when you go into a supermarket it is not unusual to see five or six different mushrooms on the shelf. When I returned to Canada my knowledge of mushrooms was elevated to a new level. The southwest coast of British Columbia supplies Europe and Japan with huge quantities of wild mushrooms. The variety available to the connoisseur is staggering, and wholesalers may offer six or seven different wild mushrooms as well as the cultivated varieties.

Chinatown is a great place to buy a variety of game birds. They add interest and complexity to menus and their rich flavors are perfect to warm the body and soul as the weather outside turns cool.

Autumn

Looking East

I could not go in

but had to bow before

this autumn-leaf temple.

—Buson

Chinese-Style Leeks Mimosa

Part of the inspiration for this variation of the classic French dish was the different kinds of Chinese preserved duck eggs. People are a little skeptical of duck eggs, covered in various unappealing substances as they are, but once you get to the egg inside, the flavor is not intimidating at all. The salted, preserved duck eggs used in this recipe are covered in what looks like coal dust but is really a salt and clay mixture. The egg retains its natural white and yellow colors. The other variety commonly available is the century or thousand-year-old egg. They are coated with a mixture of lime mud and rice bran. The white turns a translucent black color and the yolk a creamy greenish black. Try all the different varieties of preserved duck eggs to find out which you like best. They are available at Chinese markets and in some supermarkets. Chicken eggs are the logical substitute.

Prepare the eggs.

If you choose salted duck eggs, cook them as you would a hard-boiled egg. Thoroughly wash:
2 salted preserved duck eggs

Place them in boiling water and reduce the heat to a bare simmer. Cook for 10 minutes. Cool them under cold water for 5 minutes. Peel them and separate the whites from the yolks. With a spoon, push the whites through a fine sieve into a bowl. Repeat for the yolks, using a separate bowl.

If you choose thousand-year-old eggs, thoroughly wash them, then proceed from the peeling stage. You don't need to cook them.

Make a vinaigrette.

Combine in a small bowl:
2 Tbsp. (30 ml) Chinese black vinegar*
4 Tbsp. (60 ml) olive oil
1/4 tsp. (1.2 ml) salt
1/4 tsp. (1.2 ml) pepper

Set aside.

Steam:
4 large leeks, white part only
until soft but not mushy, about 10 minutes. Cut the leeks into 1" (2.5-cm) pieces, and arrange them on serving plates so they resemble their original shape. Drizzle with a spoonful of the vinaigrette and sprinkle with the sieved egg whites and egg yolks.

*See The Pantry

Serving Suggestion

Combines well with Wild Mushroom Packages (page 78) and Garlic Grilled Beef (page 84).

Leeks with Black Beans in Parchment

The funky flavor of the fermented black beans highlights the earthiness of the leeks in this recipe.

Make the black bean butter.

Combine in a bowl:
4 Tbsp. (60 ml) butter, softened
1 Tbsp. (15 ml) fermented black beans*
1 tsp. (5 ml) orange zest
1/4 tsp. (1.2 ml) pepper

Wash and cut into 1" (2.5-cm) lengths:
4 large leeks, white part only

Preheat the oven to 350°F (175°C).

Cut and lay out on your counter:
4 sheets baking parchment,
  8 1/2" x 10" (22 cm x 25 cm)

Divide the leeks among the 4 sheets of paper, arranging them in a line down the center. Top the leeks with the butter mixture.

Seal the packages by bringing the 2 long edges of the paper together. Fold the 2 edges together in narrow folds down to the level of the leeks. Fold the ends together as if you were wrapping a parcel and roll them up to seal. For some visual help with the parcels, see New Potatoes in Parchment (page 35).

Place the packages on a baking sheet and bake for 30 minutes. Serve the packages on 4 plates and enjoy the rich fragrance as they are opened at the table.

*See The Pantry

Serving Suggestion

Combines well with Chinese Greens with Spicy Miso (page 79) and Stuffed Chilies with Sancho Pepper (page 83).

Szechuan Longbeans

This is a variation of one of my favorite Chinese dishes, Szechuan green beans with pork. It features the hot, pungent flavors that are the hallmarks of Szechuan cooking. For an authentic Szechuan touch, we have used dried shrimp and preserved Chinese cabbage. You can omit them if necessary, but the dish will be less flavorful. We use Chinese longbeans here, but feel free to substitute fresh, tender green beans.

Make the shrimp mixture.

Combine in a small bowl:

1 Tbsp. (15 ml) dried shrimp, soaked for 10 minutes in warm water, drained and minced

1 Tbsp. (15 ml) finely minced ginger

1 Tbsp. (15 ml) finely minced garlic

1/4 cup (60 ml) finely minced green onions

2 Tbsp. (30 ml) preserved Chinese cabbage, minced

Make the sauce.

Combine in a small bowl:

1/4 cup (60 ml) chicken stock or dashi soup stock (see page 121)

2 Tbsp. (30 ml) balsamic vinegar

1 Tbsp. (15 ml) mushroom soy sauce

1 Tbsp. (15 ml) sugar

1/2 tsp. (2.5 ml) Vietnamese chili paste with garlic*

Wash and cut into 3" (7.5-cm) lengths:

1 lb. (450 g) Chinese longbeans

Blanch the beans in a large amount of boiling salted water. The beans should be crisp-tender but must be cooked through to release their flavor. Drain and rinse under cold running water to stop the cooking process. Drain thoroughly.

Note on Ingredients

Chinese preserved cabbage is salt-cured sui choy or napa cabbage. It is traditionally sold in brown earthenware crocks. It does not require rinsing and is pleasingly tangy in flavor.

Dried shrimp are found in every Chinese grocery store without exception. You will see them either in large open bins or in small plastic packages. They come in many sizes but all share the same funky, complex flavor that adds a traditional note to any dish in which they are used.

Mushroom soy sauce is a dark, rich-tasting soy sauce from China. It is available at all Chinese groceries and at many supermarkets. Use regular soy sauce if you can't find it.

Heat a wok or skillet. Add:

3 Tbsp. (45 ml) vegetable oil

Add the dried shrimp mixture. Stir-fry for a couple of minutes and then add the beans. Stir-fry another couple of minutes and then add the sauce. Continue stir-frying for a further minute and serve immediately.

*See The Pantry

Serving Suggestion

Combines well with Brazilian Pork-Stuffed Chilies (page 93) and Gingered Squash in Parchment (page 90).

Wild Mushroom Packages

Fall brings a profusion of mushrooms: porcini, chanterelles, matsutake, hedgehog, lobster, chicken of the woods and morels, as well as cultivated exotic varieties, such as shiitake, oyster, enoki, shimeji and cremini. Many are now available at the public market—a far cry from when I grew up in the N.W.T., where we were lucky to get a few bruised button mushrooms a week. Use as many different kinds as you can in this dish.

With a pastry brush, clean the debris from:

1 1/2 lbs. (675 g) mixed wild mushrooms

Slice the mushrooms very thinly.

Cut and lay out on your counter:

4 sheets baking parchment, 8 1/2" x 10" (22 cm x 25 cm)

Divide the mushrooms among the 4 sheets of paper, arranging them in a line down the center.

Divide:

4 Tbsp. (60 ml) butter
4 Tbsp. (60 ml) soy sauce
2 cloves garlic, minced
2 green onions, minced
2 Tbsp. (30 ml) lime juice

among the 4 packages. Sprinkle with a little:

sancho pepper*

Seal the packages by bringing the 2 long edges of the paper together. Fold the 2 edges together in narrow folds down to the level of the mushrooms. Fold the ends together as if you were wrapping a parcel and roll them up to seal. For visual help with the parcels, see New Potatoes in Parchment (page 35).

Preheat the barbecue grill or preheat the oven to 375⁰F (190⁰C). Grill or bake the packages for about 5 minutes, or until you can see bubbling and steaming inside. Put the packages onto four plates and open them at the table.

*See The Pantry

Serving Suggestion

Combines well with Chinese-Style Leeks Mimosa (page 74) and Garlic Grilled Beef (page 84).

Chinese Greens with Spicy Miso

The miso mixture dressing these greens is very versatile. It can be used as a spread for grilled or fried tofu, a dip for seafood and meat and a sauce for cooked vegetables. Use any Chinese greens that catch your eye. If you want something a little more familiar, broccoli is great with this sauce.

Make the spicy miso.

Combine in a bowl:

4 Tbsp. (60 ml) white miso*

1 Tbsp. (15 ml) mirin*

1 Tbsp. (15 ml) rice wine vinegar

1 tsp. (5 ml) sugar

1 tsp. (5 ml) Vietnamese chili paste with garlic*

Set aside.

Trim the woody ends off:

1 lb. (450 g) Chinese greens, preferably gailan

Steam the greens until crisp-tender. You can tell if the greens are done by looking at the stem end. When not quite cooked there will be a white dot in the middle of the stalk. When done, the white spot will have vanished.

Divide the greens among 4 plates. Cut them in half and spoon 1 Tbsp. (15 ml) of the spicy miso over each serving.

*See The Pantry

Serving Suggestion

Combines well with Orange-Spiced Lamb Shanks (page 96) and Yaki Onigiri (page 141).

Thai Curried Squash in Parchment

This recipe is an adaptation of a dish that a good friend of mine, Randy Enomoto, makes. It is basically a Thai curry but we have put it into parchment packages to cook. This intensifies the flavor and changes the presentation. It smells divine when the packages are opened at the table. If you are pressed for time, you can substitute a commercially prepared Thai red curry paste, but beef it up a little with some lemon grass and lime leaves if you can get them. We like to use butternut or kabocha squash in this dish because of their rich, creamy texture, but you can use any kind of winter squash.

Make a Thai red curry paste.

Combine in the bowl of a food processor:

1/2 cup (125 ml) small dried red chilies, cut in half and soaked in warm water for 20 minutes

1 tsp. (5 ml) black pepper

1 tsp. (5 ml) ground coriander

1 tsp. (5 ml) ground cumin

4 stalks lemon grass, trimmed and minced, or the zest of 3 lemons

6 sprigs cilantro

1 Tbsp. (15 ml) fresh grated ginger

1 Tbsp. (15 ml) kaffir lime leaves, minced, or the zest of 3 limes

4 cloves garlic

1 small red onion, peeled and chopped

1 tsp. (5 ml) shrimp paste*

1/2 tsp. (2.5 ml) salt

Process until smooth. This paste will keep in the fridge for a month. Use it in anything that calls for Thai red curry paste.

Make a red curry sauce.

Combine in a saucepan:

1 onion, minced

2 cloves garlic, minced

1 Tbsp. (15 ml) vegetable oil

Sweat the onions and garlic over low heat, covered, until they are soft and translucent. Remove the lid and raise the heat. Stir the mixture until it starts to brown slightly. Add:

2 Tbsp. (30 ml) Thai red curry paste

Stir for 1 minute. Add:

1 2/3 cups (410 ml) coconut milk (I prefer the Aroy-D brand from Thailand)

Simmer for 15 minutes.

Peel and cut into 1/2" (1-cm) cubes:

1 butternut or kabocha squash

You should have approximately 2 1/2 cups (625 ml).

Preheat the oven to 350°F (175°C).

Cut and lay out on your counter:
**4 sheets baking parchment,
  8 1/2" x 10" (22 cm x 25 cm)**

Divide the squash among the 4 sheets, arranging it in a line down the center.

Spoon 4 Tbsp. (60 ml) of the curry sauce into each package. Scatter over the squash:
Thai basil leaves*

Seal the packages by bringing the 2 long edges of the paper together. Fold the 2 edges together in narrow folds down to the level of the squash. Fold the ends together as if you were wrapping a parcel and roll them up to seal. Place the packages on a baking sheet and bake for 30 minutes. For some visual aid in wrapping the packages, see New Potatoes in Parchment (page 35).

*See The Pantry

Serving Suggestion

Combines well with Szechuan Longbeans (page 76) and Stuffed Chilies with Sancho Pepper (page 83).

Gailan with Mustard Butter

This recipe for mustard butter is one of our most requested. It goes well with just about any vegetable. I always think of the stronger-tasting green vegetables, like Brussels sprouts, cabbage, cauliflower and broccoli, but we have also used it very successfully with asparagus and some of the milder Chinese greens like yu choy. It is very simple and has the added bonus of keeping for a month or more in the refrigerator.

Make the mustard butter.

In a saucepan combine:

2 Tbsp. (30 ml) Dijon mustard

2 Tbsp. (30 ml) grainy Dijon mustard

1 Tbsp. (15 ml) each red and yellow mustard seeds*

1/2 lb. (225 g) butter

1 Tbsp. (15 ml) fresh lemon juice

Over low heat melt the butter and other ingredients, stirring constantly. Do not let the butter become too hot or it will separate. This is not a disaster, but try to avoid it. If it does separate, you can re-emulsify it by stirring slowly as the butter cools. When the mixture reaches a creamy, mayonnaise-like thickness, remove from the heat.

Steam:

1 large bunch of gailan

for 3-4 minutes, until it is crisp-tender.

Arrange on 4 plates or a platter. Drizzle 1/2 cup (125 ml) of the mustard butter over the gailan and serve. Store the remaining butter in the refrigerator.

*See The Pantry

Serving Suggestion

Combines well with Confit of Duck with Mango Salsa (page 94) and Smoked Salmon Roll (page 86).

Note on Ingredients

Gailan is one of the better known Chinese greens. It is sometimes called Chinese broccoli and is available at all Chinese markets.

Confit of Duck, page 94

Pappadam Curried Oysters,
page 106

Stuffed Chilies with Sancho Pepper

On a shopping trip to Chinatown, I noticed some beautiful little peppers that looked like miniature green bell peppers. We stuffed and grilled them and then I popped one into my mouth. It felt as though my mouth had caught fire! The peppers were a close relative of the habañero, the hottest pepper in the world. We decided to use jalapeños to tone down the heat of this dish.

Prepare the stuffing.

Combine in a bowl:
3/4 lb. (340 g) ground pork
2 Tbsp. (30 ml) minced green onions
2 tsp. (10 ml) grated fresh ginger
2 cloves garlic, minced
1 Tbsp. (15 ml) soy sauce
1 tsp. (5 ml) sherry
1/2 tsp. (2.5 ml) salt
1 egg
2 Tbsp. (30 ml) sesame seeds

Cover and refrigerate while you prepare:
12-16 large jalapeño chilies, cut in half, seeded and deveined*

Stuff the chili halves with the pork mixture. Mound the pork up over the edge of the peppers so they look plump and attractive.

Preheat the barbecue to medium or turn on the oven broiler and adjust the rack to 6" (15 cm) below the heat. Brush the chilies with a little:
vegetable oil

Arrange the chilies meat side down on the grill or meat side up in the oven. Cook 4-6 minutes or until the meat is well browned. Flip them over and cook for 2 more minutes. Arrange on 4 plates. Drizzle with a little:
soy sauce

To finish, sprinkle with a little:
sancho pepper*

*See The Pantry

Serving Suggestion

Combines well with Thai Curried Squash in Parchment (page 80) and Yaki Onigiri (page 141).

Garlic Grilled Beef

This beef dish is very simple but, in the way of anything made with a lot of garlic, very satisfying. We use the layers of flavor technique in this recipe, adding different garlic preparations at different stages to enhance the complexity of the finished dish. This dish has its origins in Korean cookery.

Make the marinade.

Combine in a flat dish:
2 green onions, minced
6 cloves garlic, minced
1/4 cup (60 ml) soy sauce
2 Tbsp. (30 ml) brown sugar
1 tsp. (5 ml) black pepper
2 Tbsp. (30 ml) sesame seeds
2 Tbsp. (30 ml) sesame oil

Prepare the beef.

Cut into 1" (2.5-cm) cubes:
1 1/2 lbs. (675 g) beef tenderloin

Thread the beef onto 8 bamboo skewers. Place the beef skewers in 3/4 of the marinade for 10 minutes, reserving the remaining marinade to baste the beef.

Preheat the barbecue to medium or turn on the oven broiler and adjust the rack to 6" (15 cm) below the heat. Shake the excess marinade off the skewers and barbecue or broil them for 3-5 minutes on each side, or until cooked to your liking, basting with the reserved marinade. The marinade is sweet, so be careful it doesn't burn.

Arrange 2 skewers on each of 4 plates and sprinkle the beef with:
4 Tbsp. (60 ml) Thai fried garlic*

*See The Pantry

Serving Suggestion

Combines well with Chinese-Style Leeks Mimosa (page 74) and Wild Mushroom Packages (page 78).

Autumn

Looking West

Cool night rain

brings forth

morning mushrooms.

—E. McLean

Smoked Salmon Roll

The smoked salmon roll was developed at the request of one of our best customers, Marika Sacks, who wanted a Jewish sushi roll for her son's Bar Mitzvah. We decided to eliminate the traditional rice and nori seaweed, and came up with this alternative. The salmon is rolled in an egg crêpe with asparagus and makes a beautiful mosaic pattern when cut. We use cucumber cut into strips when asparagus is not available.

Make the egg crêpes.

Whisk until well blended in a measuring cup:

5 large eggs (use 1 egg for each roll)

Heat a crêpe pan or nonstick skillet until very hot. Rub the surface of the pan with a piece of paper towel that has been dipped in a little vegetable oil. Pour in enough of the egg to coat the bottom of the pan thinly. Let the surface of the crêpe dry out a little, moving the pan around the burner to dry any very wet spots.

This will take about 20 seconds. Loosen the top edge of the crêpe from the pan with cooking chopsticks or the handle of a wooden spoon. Put the chopsticks or spoon handle across the top of the pan and flip the top edge of the crêpe up onto it. Gently pull the crêpe towards you, lifting it off the pan. When it is completely off the pan, lay the bottom edge of the crêpe at the top of the pan and put it back into the pan with the uncooked side down.

Let the crêpe dry for about 5 seconds and then turn it out onto a plate. It should only take a couple of minutes for each crêpe. This recipe makes about 5 crêpes; stack them on a plate and set them aside until you are ready to assemble the rolls. The crêpes will not stick together. For a visual aid, see the illustrations for Crab and Avocado Hoppa Rolls (page 46).

Prepare the cream cheese mixture by combining:

4 Tbsp. (60 ml) Winnipeg-style cream cheese

1 tsp. (5 ml) tiny capers, drained and minced

2 tsp. (10 ml) finely minced red onion

1 tsp. (5 ml) minced fresh dill

Set aside.

Have ready:

40 paper-thin slices lox-style smoked salmon

20 ultra-thin asparagus spears, lightly steamed

Separate the salmon slices and lay 8 in a single layer on top of each crêpe, covering it completely.

Spread a very thin 1" wide (2.5-cm) strip of the cheese mixture across the salmon near the bottom edge of the crêpes. Place 4 asparagus spears on the cream cheese. Fold the crêpes so that the asparagus is enclosed tightly on the first turn of the roll. Continue rolling into a tight roll. Using a wet, very thin-bladed knife, slice each roll into 8 equal rounds, starting at the center. Serve with the cut sides up.

Serving Suggestion

Combines well with Gailan with Mustard Butter (page 82) and Confit of Duck with Mango Salsa (page 94).

Parsnip Pancakes with Smoked Salmon

This recipe is an all-time catering favorite. It looks great on a buffet table, can be eaten hot or cold and has the cachet of smoked salmon. It also makes good use of a much undervalued vegetable, the parsnip.

Cut:

4 slices lox-style smoked salmon into strips, 1/4" x 2" (.5 cm x 5 cm).

Make the pancakes.

Peel, coarsely grate and combine in a bowl:

1 lb. (450 g) parsnips
1 small onion
1 small Granny Smith apple

Add:

1 egg
2 Tbsp. (30 ml) flour
1/2 tsp. (2.5 ml) pepper
1/2 tsp. (2.5 ml) salt
1/4 tsp. (1.2 ml) nutmeg

Mix well and form into 2" (5-cm) pancakes about 1/4" (.5 cm) thick.

Heat in a frying pan:
1 Tbsp. (15 ml) butter
1 Tbsp. (15 ml) vegetable oil

When the oil is hot sauté the pancakes over medium heat for about 2-3 minutes per side, until they are crisp and golden brown.

Arrange the pancakes on plates and top with a little dab of:
sour cream

Arrange the smoked salmon strips in an "x" pattern over the sour cream on each pancake. Garnish with:
sprigs of dill

Serving Suggestion

Combines well with Garlic Grilled Shiitake Mushrooms (page 89) and Garlic Grilled Beef (page 84).

Garlic Grilled Shiitake Mushrooms

This recipe is based on a French classic, Crêpes à la Bordelaise. It is perfect for any thick, meaty mushrooms, such as shiitakes or portabellos, but it will also work with regular button mushrooms.

Marinate the mushrooms.

Combine in a bowl:

5 cloves garlic, minced
1/2 cup (125 ml) minced parsley
1/2 cup (125 ml) extra-virgin olive oil
1/2 tsp. (2.5 ml) pepper
1/4 tsp. (1.2 ml) salt
12-16 large shiitake mushrooms, stems removed

Toss the mushrooms with the other ingredients until thoroughly coated. Marinate for 20 minutes.

Preheat the barbecue to medium or turn on the oven broiler and adjust the rack to 3" (7.5 cm) below the heat. Arrange the mushrooms cap side down on the grill or oven rack. Cook 2-3 minutes, or until a few drops of moisture form. Flip them over and cook for 1 more minute. Arrange on 4 plates and serve immediately.

Serving Suggestion

Combines well with Parsnip Pancakes with Smoked Salmon (page 88) and Confit of Duck with Mango Salsa (page 94).

Gingered Squash in Parchment

Cooking in parchment paper combines the best of steaming with the ease of baking. These packages are opened at the table, treating everyone to a flood of wonderful aromas that are the essence of autumn. Any kind of winter squash works well, but butternut and kabocha have an especially creamy texture.

Serving Suggestion

Combines well with Garlic Grilled Beef (page 84), and Yaki Onigiri (page 141) for a simple, soul-satisfying meal.

Preheat the oven to 350ºF (175ºC).

Peel and cut into 3/4" (2-cm) cubes:
1 butternut or kabocha squash

You should have approximately 2 1/2 cups (625 ml).

Cut and lay out on your counter:
**4 sheets baking parchment,
    8 1/2" x 10" (22 cm x 25 cm)**

Divide the squash among the 4 sheets of paper, arranging it in a line down the center.

Have ready:
**zest and juice of 1 orange
1 Tbsp. (15 ml) grated fresh
    ginger
2 tsp. (10 ml) butter
4 Tbsp. (60 ml) whipping cream
4 tsp. (20 ml) Demerara brown
    sugar
4 sprigs coriander**

Divide the assembled ingredients among the 4 packages. To each add:
pinch salt and pepper

Seal the packages by bringing the long edges of the paper together. Fold the two edges together in narrow folds down to the level of the squash. Fold the ends together as if you were wrapping a parcel and roll them up to seal. For a visual aid, see the illustrations for New Potatoes in Parchment (page 35).

Place on a baking sheet and bake for 30 minutes.

Chinese Ratatouille

This is a ratatouille by virtue of the fact that it includes eggplant and zucchini. It is very popular, especially with one of our long-time waitresses, Theresa Fidel. It is the perfect "rice puller," a dish that is great on top of a bowl of rice. In the Chinese style, it is a good idea to do the cleaning and cutting of the vegetables before you start cooking.

Serving Suggestion

Combines well with Scallops with Lily Butter (page 92) and Orange-Spiced Lamb Shanks (page 96).

Combine in a small bowl:

8 cloves garlic, minced

1 small onion, cut into 1/4" (.5-cm) dice

1/4 cup (60 ml) minced fresh ginger

Combine in a large bowl:

1 eggplant, cut into 1/2" (1-cm) cubes

1 red bell pepper, cut into 1/4" (.5-cm) dice

4 shiitake mushrooms, stems removed and cut into quarters

Combine in another large bowl:

1 large zucchini, cut into 1/2" (1-cm) cubes

1/4 lb. (115 g) firm tofu, cut into 1/2" (1-cm) cubes

1 small Chinese fuzzy melon, washed and cut into 1/2" (1-cm) cubes (optional)

Heat a large sauté pan until quite hot. Add:

3 Tbsp. (45 ml) vegetable oil

1 Tbsp. (15 ml) sesame oil

Heat for a further 30 seconds. Add the garlic mixture to the pan and stir-fry for 1 minute. Add the eggplant mixture and stir-fry for 2 minutes. Add:

1/4 cup (60 ml) dry sherry

1/2 cup (125 ml) hoisin sauce*

1/2 cup (125 ml) oyster sauce

1/2 cup (125 ml) water

Reduce the heat to medium. Stir to combine everything in the pan. Cover and simmer for 15 minutes. Check the pan every couple of minutes and give it a stir. If the mixture starts to stick, add a little water. Stir in the zucchini mixture and cook for a further 5-10 minutes, or until the zucchini is cooked but not mushy.

Stir in:

1 tsp. (5 ml) Vietnamese chili paste with garlic*

Serve in small bowls topped with a few:

cilantro leaves, chopped

*See The Pantry

Note on Ingredients

Chinese fuzzy melons are one of a variety of summer squashes that are available at Chinese markets. They look a lot like hairy zucchinis. Wash and cook them as you would any summer squash. The fuzz will disappear with cooking.

Scallops with Lily Butter

The lily butter in this recipe is a variation on the French classic Beurre Blanc sauce. This version uses dried lily buds, the unopened flower buds of a type of Chinese day lily. They are very popular with vegetarians in China. Their sweet, smoky flavor perfectly complements the sweetness of the scallops. If you can't find the lily buds, which are available at most Chinese groceries, substitute sundried tomatoes.

Make the lily butter.

Combine in a small saucepan:

3 dried lily buds
1/2 cup (125 ml) white wine
2 Tbsp. (30 ml) minced white onion

Bring the wine mixture to a boil and reduce it to 2 Tbsp. (30 ml). Put it into the bowl of a food processor and add:

1/2 cup (125 ml) butter, cut into small cubes

Process until smooth. Set aside.

Thread:

16 jumbo scallops
on 4 bamboo skewers.

Preheat the barbecue to high or turn on the oven broiler and adjust the rack to 3" (7.5 cm) below the heat. Barbecue or broil the skewers for 2-3 minutes on each side, or until just done. Do not overcook them or they will be tough and will lose a lot of flavor. Serve the scallops on a pool of the lily butter.

Serving Suggestion

Combines well with Chinese Ratatouille (page 91) and Yaki Onigiri (page 141).

Brazilian Pork-Stuffed Chilies

This recipe was inspired by a recipe from Mark Miller's Coyote Cafe Cookbook. I adapted it to continue a line of stuffed chilies that I was developing. The cooking liquid is intensely clove-flavored. With the fruit, garlic and savory herbs, this makes a very interesting dish.

Serving Suggestion

Combines well with Szechuan Longbeans (page 76) and Gingered Squash in Parchment (page 90).

Heat your barbecue to medium or turn on the oven broiler and adjust the rack to 6" (15 cm) below the heat.

Rub:

4 green Anaheim chilies*
4 red Anaheim chilies*

with a little oil and grill or broil them, turning them until the skin on each side is black and blistered. Place them in a plastic bag to cool for 15 minutes. Remove the peppers from the bag and peel off the skin. Make a slit down one side of each pepper. Snip the seed ball near the stem with a pair of kitchen scissors and pull out the seeds. Dip the peppers in a bowl of water to remove any seeds that remain. Pat dry.

Heat a sauté pan and add:

3 Tbsp. (45 ml) vegetable oil
5 cloves garlic, peeled and minced
2 jalapeño chilies, minced, seeds in*

Sauté for a minute. Add:

1 lb. (450 g) ground pork shoulder

Sauté until the pork is completely cooked. Add:

1 cup (250 ml) orange juice
2 tsp. (10 ml) ground cloves
1 Tbsp. (15 ml) dried oregano
1 tsp. (5 ml) ground cumin
1 tsp. (5 ml) ground coriander
1 tsp. (5 ml) ground allspice
1 bay leaf
1 tsp. (5 ml) black pepper
1/2 tsp. (2.5 ml) salt
2 Tbsp. (30 ml) soy sauce
2 Tbsp. (30 ml) brown sugar

Cook until the liquid is almost all absorbed, stirring constantly.

Divide the pork mixture between 4 plates, arranging it in 2 rows about the length of the peppers.

Set out:

32 fresh oregano leaves

and place 4 on each row. Place a green chili over one row and a red over the other on each plate. Tuck the edges of the peppers under the pork to make them look like whole peppers. Garnish with:

sprigs of oregano

*See The Pantry

Confit of Duck with Mango Salsa

Confit of duck was one of those dishes that struck just the right kind of chord during the long northern winters. It is a labor of love as there are several steps involved in the preparation, but it adds an incredible depth of flavor to any dish it is used in. It is also just plain delicious to eat on its own. Confit must be made in large quantities to ensure that the duck cooks long and slow as opposed to frying. Use any duck not used in this recipe in soups or as part of a composed salad. I have reduced the amount of salt substantially from the traditional recipe, so this will not keep for more than a couple of weeks in your fridge.

To make confit you need a large amount of rendered duck fat. You should be able to order duck skin and fat scraps from your butcher.

Place:

4 lbs. (1800 g) duck scraps

in a large pot. Boil it with a couple of inches (5 cm) of water for an hour. Strain the liquid into another large bowl and put it in the fridge to solidify overnight. Discard the skin and other fat scraps that are left in the pan.

The next day remove and reserve the solidified fat from the bowl and discard any juices left in the bottom. The fat will keep indefinitely in the freezer. Once you use it for making confit it will keep for a week or 2 in the fridge covering the duck pieces. After you have used all of the duck, freeze the fat until the next time you make confit. Your rendered duck fat is a valuable cooking resource, so try to save as much as you can when you are taking the duck out of the fat. You will need 6 cups (1.5 l) of rendered duck fat for this recipe.

Make the duck salt.

Combine in a jar:

1 cup (250 ml) salt
1/4 cup (60 ml) pepper
2 Tbsp. (30 ml) dried thyme
1/2 tsp. (2.5 ml) ground allspice
1/2 tsp. (2.5 ml) ground cloves
1 tsp. (5 ml) ground cumin
1 tsp. (5 ml) ground Szechuan peppercorns*
1 tsp. (5 ml) ground coriander

Cut into 8 pieces each:
2 whole ducks

You can have your butcher do the cutting for you or you might even want to order eight duck legs and cut them into thighs and drumsticks. You should have 16 pieces of duck in all. Rub each duck piece with 1 tsp. (5 ml) of the salt mixture. Put them into a colander over a large bowl, cover and refrigerate overnight.

Melt 6 cups (1.5 l) of the rendered duck fat in a large Dutch oven or stockpot. Add the duck pieces and:

1 head of garlic, unpeeled, cut in half horizontally
2 bay leaves

Turn the heat to low and let the duck slowly come to a simmer. The surface of the fat should just be trembling, with the occasional bubble breaking the surface. If the fat boils rapidly, the duck will be tough. Simmer for 1 1/2 hours, or until the duck is very tender. Turn off the heat and let the duck cool in the fat. When the fat is room temperature, transfer the duck to a container that will fit in your fridge. Pour the duck fat over the duck. Try to leave any dark liquid in the pan and discard it. Refrigerate the duck for a couple of days before using it. The fat will solidify around the pieces of duck and will have to be scraped off before the duck can be finished.

On the day you are going to serve the duck, make the mango salsa.

Combine in a bowl:

1 mango, cut off the stone, peeled and cut into 1/2" (1-cm) cubes
12 mint leaves, minced
1 tsp. (5 ml) lime juice
1/4 tsp. (1.2 ml) sugar (if needed)
salt and pepper to taste
1/2 jalapeño chili, seeded and minced*
1 Tbsp. (15 ml) minced red onion

Set aside.

Remove 4 pieces of duck from the fat, scraping as much fat as you can back into the container. Heat the barbecue to medium or turn on the broiler and adjust the oven rack to 6" (15 cm) beneath the element. Grill the duck for 3 minutes on each side, or until the skin is nice and crisp. Arrange the duck on serving plates and put a large spoonful of the mango salsa beside each piece.

*See The Pantry

Serving Suggestion
Combines well with Garlic Grilled Shiitake Mushrooms (page 89) and Parsnip Pancakes with Smoked Salmon (page 88).

Orange-Spiced Lamb Shanks

This lamb dish fuses the Chinese art of slow cooking with the western love of barbecue. The shanks are braised for 3 hours to flavor and tenderize them. They are then finished on the grill to give them a crisp exterior and a smoky flavor.

Serving Suggestion

Combines well with Smoked Salmon Roll (page 86) and Chinese Greens with Spicy Miso (page 79).

Combine in a pot large enough to hold them comfortably:

4 lamb shanks
1/2 cup (125 ml) soy sauce
1/2 cup (125 ml) brown sugar
1/2 cup (125 ml) orange juice
zest of 2 oranges
1 cinnamon stick
10 star anise seeds
1 Tbsp. (15 ml) whole allspice
2" (5-cm) chunk of ginger, cut into pieces
5 cloves garlic, crushed

Add enough water to cover by 1" (2.5 cm) and bring the mixture to a boil. Turn the heat to low and simmer, covered, for 3 hours. The shanks should be very tender.

Remove them from the broth and let them cool slightly. The shanks can be prepared to this point days in advance and refrigerated.

Make the ginger aioli.

Combine in the bowl of a food processor:

1 egg yolk
1 heaping tsp. (6 ml) Dijon mustard
1 heaping tsp. (6 ml) garlic purée (see page 117)
1 tsp. (5 ml) vinegar

With the processor running, add, in a very thin stream or drop by drop:

3/4 cup (185 ml) vegetable oil

When all of the oil has been amalgamated and the mixture looks like mayonnaise, add:

1 1/2 tsp. (7.5 ml) minced fresh ginger
juice of 1 lemon

Process again and add:

1/2 cup (125 ml) vegetable oil, in a thin stream

When the oil has been emulsified, add:

3/4 cup (185 ml) parsley leaves
1/4 tsp. (1.2 ml) salt

Process until the parsley is almost puréed and the sauce is a green color.

To finish the shanks, preheat the barbecue grill to medium-high or turn on the broiler and adjust the oven rack to 6" (15 cm) below the heat. Grill or broil the shanks for 3-4 minutes on each side, or until the marrow in the bone is bubbling. Serve on individual plates with a heaping spoonful of the ginger aioli draped across the center of the lamb. Garnish with a sprig of rosemary or thyme if you have them.

Winter

I have a special attachment to the food of winter, having spent so much of my life in the long winters of the Northwest Territories. Dishes prepared at this time of year are substantial, complex and full of flavor. Hearty soups, stews and casseroles immediately come to mind, as do richer, more intensely flavored game meats and the peppery, robust greens of the cabbage family. A particular favorite in Fort Smith was the French classic, Cassoulet: a bean casserole with lamb, pork, duck confit and various kinds of sausages. When the two- to three-day process was finished and that big orange Dutch oven was sitting on our dining room table, still bubbling, sending sublime aromas wafting through the house, my family was in culinary heaven. Winter food should be comfort food.

Winter

Looking East

They spoke no word,

the guest, the host,

and the white chrysanthemum.

—Author unknown

Korean Spiced Salmon with Crispy Noodles

I saw a recipe for Noodle Pillows in Barbara Tropp's great cookbook, The China Moon Cookbook. *It inspired this recipe for a salmon sashimi, using the crisp noodles as a platform for the cold, soft salmon. The juxtaposition of hot and cold, crisp and soft in this recipe is thrilling.*

Make the sauce.

Combine in a bowl:
1 cup (250 ml) soy sauce
1/2 cup (125 ml) sugar
1" (2.5-cm) piece ginger, grated
3 cloves garlic, minced
1 tsp. (5 ml) Vietnamese chili paste with garlic*
1 Tbsp. (15 ml) sesame oil

This makes more sauce than you need, but it keeps a long time in the fridge and is great with sushi or on stir-fried vegetables.

Make the noodle cakes.

Bring a pot of water to the boil. Add:
2 bundles somen noodles*

Cook until soft. Oil a small cookie sheet. Drain the noodles and quickly form them into 6" (15-cm) pancakes on the cookie sheet. Cover and put them into the refrigerator to set. These can be made a day ahead.

Just before serving, heat a sauté pan with:
1 cup (250 ml) vegetable oil
to 350ºF (175ºC). (Use a candy or deep-fry thermometer to check the temperature of the oil.) Add the noodle cakes and fry them on both sides until crisp and golden.

Drain on a paper towel.

Prepare the salmon.

Cut into small cubes and place in a bowl:
2 6-oz. (180-g) filet pieces of raw, sashimi-grade salmon*

Add 5 Tbsp. (75 ml) of the sauce and:
1 green onion, finely chopped
2 Tbsp. (30 ml) toasted pine nuts

Toss to combine.

Put one noodle cake on each of 4 plates. Top with a generous pile of the salmon mixture.

Garnish with a sprinkle of:
black and white sesame seeds

*See The Pantry

Serving Suggestion

Combines well with Grilled Mochi with Nori (page 104) and Bombay Barbecue Chicken (page 111).

Sweet Potato with Soy Butter

Grilled corn on the cob and yams are traditional fall and winter festival fare in Japan. You can find them at numerous outdoor stalls wherever an event is being staged. Every time I cook these I am reminded of the outdoor dancing, singing and feasting that are the essence of the Japanese festival season.

Wash and cut into 1/2" (1-cm) disks:
1 large sweet potato
1 large yam

Put them in a pot and cover with water. Bring to a boil and cook for about 10 minutes. They should be completely cooked, that is, soft to an inserted skewer, as they will not soften any further when they are grilled. Drain and cool.

Make the soy butter.

Soften:
1/4 cup (60 ml) butter

Add:
1 1/2 tsp. (7.5 ml) soy sauce

Stir until it is emulsified.

Preheat the barbecue to medium or turn on the broiler and adjust oven rack to 6" (15 cm) beneath the heat. Brush the sweet potato and yam rounds with a little oil. Grill or broil for about 3 minutes on each side. Serve with some soy butter spooned onto each round.

Sprinkle with a little:
sancho pepper*

*See The Pantry

Serving Suggestion

Combines well with Red Snapper with Garlic Ancho Chili Spread (page 122) and Chicken Livers with Soy and Sancho (page 112).

Mustard Greens with Karashi Miso

When we were staying in Japan I was fortunate to be introduced to the second head chef at the Imperial Palace, and he invited us to his house for dinner. One of the stand-out dishes he prepared that night was a simple sautéed pork with this karashi miso. Karashi translates as "mustard." I like the idea of serving the same product in different forms, hence the mustard greens with the mustard sauce.

Make the karashi miso.

Combine in a bowl:

4 Tbsp. (60 ml) white miso*

1 Tbsp. (15 ml) mirin*

1 Tbsp. (15 ml) rice wine vinegar*

1 tsp. (5 ml) sugar

2 tsp. (10 ml) Dijon mustard

Set aside.

Trim the woody ends off:

1 lb. (450 g) Chinese mustard greens

Cut the thick leaves into 2 or 3 pieces and set aside.

Steam the greens, placing the thick pieces on the bottom and the leafy greens on top, until crisp-tender. You can tell if the greens are done by looking at the stem end of one of the thick pieces. If not quite done, it will have a white dot in the middle. When it is done, the white spot will have vanished.

Divide the greens among 4 plates, and spoon 1 Tbsp. (15 ml) of the karashi miso onto each serving.

*See The Pantry

Serving Suggestion

Combines well with Grilled Mochi with Nori (page 104) and Black Cod Kasu Yaki (page 110).

Note on Ingredients

Mustard greens are called *gai choy* by the Chinese. They are perhaps the favorite vegetable in the repertoire for turning into pickles. Fresh, they have a rich texture and flavor, perfect for using in soup and with strong sauces. They are available in Chinese markets. Interesting substitutes are Belgian endive or the more readily available sui choy or napa cabbage.

Tamarind Spiced Green Beans

This is an adaptation of an Indonesian dish. The original calls for long cooking of the beans, but we tend to lean more towards brevity in the cooking process. That said, green beans are one of those vegetables that need to be cooked long enough to develop their natural sweetness. Always look for slender, smallish, tender beans as opposed to the large ones, which are inevitably tough and woody.

Make the tamarind sauce.

Combine in a sauté pan:

1 medium onion, coarsely chopped
4 cloves garlic, chopped
3 jalapeño chilies, stem removed, chopped*
1 tsp. (5 ml) shrimp paste*
1 tsp. (5 ml) salt
2 Tbsp. (30 ml) vegetable oil

Sauté over medium heat until the vegetables are softened.

Put the mixture into the bowl of a food processor. Add:

2 Tbsp. (30 ml) sesame oil
2 Tbsp. (30 ml) Thai fish sauce*
1 tsp. (5 ml) Vietnamese chili paste with garlic*
2 Tbsp. (30 ml) tamarind concentrate or softened tamarind pulp*

Process until smooth. Set aside.

Wash, top and tail:

1 lb. (450 g) green beans

Steam until they are crisp-tender, approximately 4-5 minutes.

Heat:

2 Tbsp. (30 ml) vegetable oil

in a large sauté pan until hot. Add the beans and 1/2 cup (125 ml) of the sauce. Stir-fry for 30 seconds and turn out onto 4 plates.

Garnish with:

Thai crisp fried onions*

*See The Pantry

Serving Suggestion

Combines well with Jumbo Prawns with Creole Butter (page 120) and Korean Buffalo Osso Bucco (page 114).

Grilled Mochi with Nori

Mochi is a ground rice cake that is eaten at New Year celebrations in Japan. It was traditionally made by dumping a large quantity of cooked, glutinous rice into a huge bowl and then letting two or three young men hammer away at it with large poles until it formed a smooth, chewy cake. It has a very interesting texture and does wild things when you grill or broil it. Mochi and nori seaweed are available at all Japanese groceries. There is no substitute, but Yaki Onigiri (page 141) makes a great stand-in dish.

Make the tare yaki sauce (see page 17).

Preheat the barbecue to medium-high or turn on the broiler and adjust the oven rack to 6" (15 cm) beneath the heat.

Set out:
4 pieces mochi
1 sheet nori seaweed, cut into 4 strips, 1" x 6" (2.5 cm x 15 cm)

Brush the mochi with a little oil. Grill or broil for 3 minutes on each side, or until it is puffed and golden. Dip the mochi in tare yaki sauce and then wrap one of the nori strips around each piece.

Sprinkle with a little:
sancho pepper*

*See The Pantry

Serving Suggestion
Combines well with Mustard Greens with Karashi Miso (page 102) and Black Cod Kasu Yaki (page 110).

Hot and Sour Tofu Packages

A variation on our popular tofu packages, the recipe for the sauce in this dish is derived from Chinese hot and sour soup. Baby corn, peas, green soy beans and mochi all make good alternative stuffing ingredients.

Serving Suggestion

Combines well with Curried Seafood Hotpot (page 108) and Yaki Onigiri (page 141).

Make the hot and sour sauce.

Combine in a medium pot:

1 Tbsp. (15 ml) hot chili flakes
3 cloves garlic
1 cup (250 ml) rice wine vinegar*
1/4 cup (60 ml) sugar
2 Tbsp. (30 ml) soy sauce
2 Tbsp. (30 ml) chopped fresh ginger
1/4 cup (60 ml) mirin*
1 tsp. (5 ml) salt

Bring the mixture to a boil and cook for 15 minutes.

Mix:

1 Tbsp. (15 ml) cornstarch
2 Tbsp. (30 ml) cold water

Stir the cornstarch mixture into the hot sauce. The sauce should thicken slightly. Cook 2 more minutes. Strain into a bowl.

Prepare the tofu puffs.

Bring a large pot of water to a boil. Put:

1 package deep-fried tofu puffs (6-8 puffs)*

into the boiling water and cover with a lid that is slightly smaller than the pot to make sure they are submerged. Boil for 10 minutes. This removes excess oil from the puffs. Drain the puffs and let them cool.

Prepare the packages.

Assemble the following ingredients:

1 large carrot, cut into 2" (5-cm) lengths and julienned
1 piece flavored dried tofu, cut into 1" (2.5-cm) squares*
8 fresh water chestnuts, peeled*
1 green onion, cut into 2" (5-cm) lengths

Blanch the carrots until crisp-tender, about 4 minutes. Drain and run under cold water to cool.

With a knife or pair of scissors, cut a slit along one edge of the tofu puffs. Work your finger into the slit until you have a small pouch, taking care not to rip the sides or bottom of the puff. Divide the assembled ingredients equally among the tofu puffs and stuff them.

Heat your barbecue to medium-high or turn on the broiler and adjust the oven rack to 6" (15 cm) below the heat. Grill or broil the packages on a baking sheet for 4 minutes on each side.

Dip the cooked packages into the hot and sour sauce. Drain the excess and serve, sprinkled with:

sancho pepper*

*See The Pantry

Pappadam Curried Oysters

When I was 11 years old, a family vacation took us to Vancouver Island. It was the first time I had ever seen the ocean or eaten fresh seafood. My dad brought back a dozen oysters to our cabin and breaded and fried them. I was very impressed. Since then I have tried oysters in many guises but one of my favorites features coarse-ground raw pappadams as the breading and two Indian-style accompaniments—a raita and an onion salad.

Make the cucumber raita.

Quarter lengthwise and slice thinly:
1/4 English cucumber

Put the slices into a strainer and sprinkle them with:
1/2 tsp. (2.5 ml) salt

Toss the slices to distribute the salt and then let them drain over the sink for 20 minutes.

Combine in a small sauté pan:
1/4 tsp. (1.2 ml) black mustard seeds*
1/4 tsp. (1.2 ml) ground coriander
1/4 tsp. (1.2 ml) ground cumin

Toast the spices over high heat for 10 seconds. Put them in a medium-sized bowl and add:
1/2 cup (125 ml) yoghurt
1/4 tsp. (1.2 ml) sugar
1/2 clove garlic, minced
1/4 tsp. (1.2 ml) fresh grated ginger
1/2 tsp. (2.5 ml) lemon juice

Stir to combine. Add the cucumber to the yoghurt mixture. Set aside.

Make the onion salad.

Peel and thinly slice:
1 small red onion

Heat in a sauté pan until very hot, almost smoking:
1 tsp. (5 ml) vegetable oil

Add the sliced onion and stir-fry for 1 minute to soften slightly. Put the onion in a sieve and place under cold running water to stop the cooking process. Drain.

In a small bowl mix together:
2 Tbsp. (30 ml) balsamic vinegar
1 Tbsp. (15 ml) brown sugar
3 sun-dried tomatoes, diced
1 tsp. (5 ml) grated fresh ginger
1 jalapeño chili, seeded and minced*
2 Tbsp. (30 ml) chopped fresh coriander leaves
salt to taste

Add the onion. Mix well and chill.

Put into the bowl of a food processor:
3 uncooked pappadams, broken into 1" (2.5-cm) pieces

Process them until they are ground into pieces the size of grains of rice. Pour into a bowl.

Blot dry on paper toweling:

8 large oysters, shucked

Dredge the oysters in the ground pappadams. Make sure they are well coated. Heat in a large sauté pan until medium hot:

4 Tbsp. (60 ml) vegetable oil

2 Tbsp. (30 ml) butter, preferably clarified or unsalted

Add the oysters and sauté until they are crisp and golden on each side, about 3 minutes per side. Drain for a few seconds on paper towel to get rid of excess oil and then transfer them to 4 plates. Garnish with the cucumber raita and onion salad.

*See The Pantry

Serving Suggestion

Combines well with Eggplant with Garlic and Goat Cheese (page 117) and Persian Honey-Spiced Chicken (page 123).

Curried Seafood Hotpot

Hotpots are perfect winter food, the complex aromas mingled in an earthenware pot and released with a flourish as the lid is lifted. Nothing could be more satisfying. This dish is an adaptation of laksa, a hotpot from Malaysia. It features a variety of seafood in a curried coconut broth. The fish stock recipe makes more than you need for this dish, so freeze any you don't use. If you are pressed for time, you can substitute clam nectar or Japanese dashi soup stock for the fish stock. The rice stick noodles can be replaced with any kind of pasta.

Make the fish stock.

Combine in a large pot:

1 onion, coarsely chopped
1 stalk celery, coarsely chopped
2 carrots, coarsely chopped
1 small fennel bulb with the
    fronds, coarsely chopped
1 large leek, coarsely chopped
4 cloves garlic, coarsely chopped
1/4 cup (60 ml) olive oil

Sauté the vegetables until slightly softened.

Add:

2 rockfish heads or fish bones,
    chopped into 2" (5-cm) pieces
    and washed
1 Tbsp. (15 ml) fennel seed
1 Tbsp. (15 ml) peppercorns
2 bay leaves
2 quarts (2 l) water

Bring the stock to a simmer and simmer it gently for 30 minutes, skimming off the foam that rises to the surface. Strain the stock through a fine mesh strainer into a container. Reserve the liquid and discard the solids.

Make the coconut curry sauce.

Mix 2 cups (500 ml) of the fish stock with:

1 3/4 cups (435 ml) coconut milk
1 Tbsp. (15 ml) brown sugar
1 Tbsp. (15 ml) soy sauce
1 tsp. (5 ml) rice wine vinegar*
2 Tbsp. (30 ml) Indian curry
    paste or powder

Bring to a boil and cook for 15 minutes. Set aside.

Assemble the hotpot.

Cut into narrow strips:

1 small red bell pepper
1 small yellow bell pepper
1 small onion
1 small fennel bulb

Sauté the vegetables until soft in:

3 Tbsp. (45 ml) olive oil

Cook:

1 1/4-lb. (110-g) package Thai or
    Vietnamese rice stick noodles

in boiling water until just done, still slightly firm to the bite. Drain and rinse under cold water to prevent further cooking.

Arrange the noodles in the bottom of a large Japanese- or Chinese-style hotpot. (You can substitute a regular soup pot, but the presentation will not be as spectacular.) Arrange the sautéed vegetables on top of the noodles. Arrange on top of the vegetables:

1 1/2-lb. (225-g) filet of rock fish, cut into 8 pieces

12 clams, rinsed

12 mussels, debearded and rinsed

8 small calamari, cleaned and sliced into 1/2" (1-cm) rings

4 pink scallops, rinsed

8 prawns, peeled

A few leaves of kale, trimmed of large veins and sliced into ribbons 1/2" (1 cm) wide.

Pour enough coconut curry sauce into the pot to cover the vegetables and fish. It should be an inch (2.5 cm) below the lip of the pot. Bring it to a boil. Cover and cook for 2 minutes, or until the mussels and clams open.

*See The Pantry

Serving Suggestion

Combines well with Hot and Sour Tofu Packages (page 105) and Spicy Shrimp Onigiri (page 142).

Black Cod Kasu Yaki

Kasu is the lees from making sake. During the process, rice is treated with an enzyme called koji, which transforms the starches in the rice into fermentable sugars. When yeast and water are added to the mixture, it ferments into sake. The liquid is then drawn off and the solids are pressed into a cake, called kasu. Buddhist monks in Japan grill it and eat it straight up. Most people use it as the basis for a marinade, as we do in this recipe. You can get it in Japanese grocery stores. There is no substitute, but an equally good marinade can be made by omitting it and tripling the amount of white miso in the recipe.

Combine in the bowl of a food processor:

1/2 cup (125 ml) kasu
1/4 cup (60 ml) sake
1/4 cup (60 ml) white miso*

Process until smooth.

In a bowl, combine the kasu mixture with:

4 6-oz. (180-g) filets of black cod

Marinate for 1 to 2 hours.

Preheat your barbecue to medium-high or turn on the broiler and adjust the oven rack to 6" (15 cm) below the heat.

Wash the kasu mixture off the cod filets under running water and blot dry. Grill or broil the fish for 2-3 minutes on each side, or until it is done to your liking. Remove to 4 plates and garnish with a small pile of:

pickled ginger*

*See The Pantry

Serving Suggestion

Combines well with Mustard Greens with Karashi Miso (page 102) and Grilled Mochi with Nori (page 104).

Bombay Barbecue Chicken

Indian spices and the barbecue are a natural match. Much of the cooking in India is done over an open fire, so this comes as no surprise. These chicken skewers are bathed in a traditional yoghurt-based marinade. We serve them with pappadams and crisp fried onions.

Serving Suggestion

Combines well with Korean Spiced Salmon with Crispy Noodles (page 100) and Yaki Onigiri (page 141).

Make the marinade.

Combine in the bowl of a food processor:

1 small onion

3 cloves garlic, minced

1 Tbsp. (15 ml) minced fresh ginger

1/2 cup (125 ml) fresh cilantro

Process until smooth. Heat in a medium-sized pot:

1 1/2 Tbsp. (22 ml) vegetable oil

Add:

1 tsp. (5 ml) turmeric

1 1/2 Tbsp. (22 ml) garam masala

1/2 tsp. (2.5 ml) chili powder

1/2 tsp. (2.5 ml) salt

Stir-fry the spices for 30 seconds. Add the onion mixture and cook for about 5 minutes. Add:

1 cup (250 ml) yoghurt

1/4 cup (60 ml) sun-dried tomatoes, diced

Cook for 10 more minutes, stirring to prevent scorching, or until the mixture thickens slightly. Set aside.

Cut into 1" (2.5-cm) cubes:

4 skinless chicken breasts or 6 boneless thighs

Thread the chicken onto 8 bamboo skewers. Place the skewers in a flat bowl and cover with 1 cup (250 ml) of the marinade. Marinate the chicken for at least 30 minutes. Reserve the remaining marinade for basting and to drizzle on the cooked chicken.

Preheat your barbecue to medium or turn on the broiler and adjust the oven rack to 6" (15 cm) beneath the heat. Shake the excess marinade off the skewers and barbecue or broil them for 3-5 minutes on each side, or until thoroughly cooked. Be careful that the chicken doesn't burn, a risk with any yoghurt-based marinade.

Divide the skewers among 4 plates. Drizzle the reserved marinade over the chicken and sprinkle with:

1/4 cup (60 ml) coarsely chopped mint leaves

1/4 cup (60 ml) crisp fried onions*

*See The Pantry

Chicken Livers with Soy and Sancho

Chicken livers and other innards are a "love 'em or hate 'em" proposition. I happen to love them. Most people who put aside prejudice and try this version of chicken livers tend to love them as well.

Make the marinade.

Combine in a bowl:
1/3 cup (80 ml) mirin*
2 Tbsp. (30 ml) soy sauce
1/4 cup (60 ml) sake

Add:
1/2 lb. (225 g) fresh, whole chicken livers

Marinate the livers for 1 hour.

Thread the livers onto 8 bamboo skewers. Preheat the barbecue to medium-high or turn on the broiler and adjust the oven rack to 6" (15 cm) below the heat. Grill or broil the livers for about 3 minutes per side. They should be slightly pink inside.

Remove to 4 plates and drizzle with a little:
soy sauce

Finish with a sprinkle of:
sancho pepper*

*See The Pantry

Serving Suggestion

Combines well with Mustard Greens with Karashi Miso (page 102) and Sweet Potato with Soy Butter (page 101).

Kashmiri Curried Beef

The Kashmiri masala that we use in this recipe is very heavy on the garlic and spice. This is in contrast to the style of cooking practiced by the Kashmiri Brahmins, who do not eat garlic or onions, which are thought to inflame the baser passions. Obviously, the common people of Kashmir were not too concerned about this!

The Kashmiri masala paste is a type of curry paste, infinitely more interesting and flavorful than ordinary curry powder. It is carried in many supermarkets, but you can use curry powder in a pinch.

Serving Suggestion

Combines well with Chinese Greens with Black Olives (page 116) and Oyster and Bacon Yaki (page 119).

Make the marinade.

Combine in a flat dish:
6 cloves garlic, minced
2 tsp. (10 ml) ground coriander
1 tsp. (5 ml) garam masala
1 tsp. (5 ml) ground cumin
1/2 tsp. (2.5 ml) ground ginger
1/2 tsp. (2.5 ml) ground turmeric
1/8 tsp. (.5 ml) ground nutmeg
1 tsp. (5 ml) salt
1 Tbsp. (15 ml) vegetable oil

Cut into 1" (2.5-cm) cubes:
1 1/2 lbs. (675 g) beef tenderloin

Thread the beef onto 8 bamboo skewers. Coat the beef thoroughly with the marinade and marinate for 2 hours.

Make the curry sauce.

Heat in a saucepan:
2 Tbsp. (30 ml) vegetable oil

Add:
1 small onion, finely chopped
4 cloves garlic, finely minced
1 small stick cinnamon
1/4 tsp. (1.2 ml) ground cardamom
pinch of ground cloves
1 Tbsp. (15 ml) Kashmiri masala paste

Sauté the mixture over medium-low heat until the onion starts to brown. Add:
1/2 cup (125 ml) water

Simmer covered over low heat for 15 minutes. Stir occasionally to make sure it doesn't scorch. Add:
1/2 tsp. (2.5 ml) cumin seeds, toasted
1/2 tsp. (2.5 ml) garam masala
1/2 cup (125 ml) yoghurt

Cook for 2 more minutes, stirring constantly. Set aside.

Preheat the barbecue to medium or turn on the broiler and adjust the oven rack to 6" (15 cm) below the heat. Shake the excess marinade off the skewers and barbecue or broil them for 3-5 minutes on each side, or until cooked to your liking. Arrange the skewers on individual plates, 2 per plate. Spoon some of the curry sauce over them and sprinkle with:
4 Tbsp. (60 ml) Thai fried garlic*
1 jalapeño chili, seeded and finely minced*
2 Tbsp. (30 ml) chopped cilantro leaves

*See The Pantry

Korean Buffalo Osso Bucco

No, the buffalo is not Korean! Rather, this is one of those cross-cultural experiments we are famous for. The buffalo shanks are braised in a Korean-style broth, grilled and topped with a spicy sesame-oil-spiked mayonnaise. Ask your butcher to cut the shanks osso bucco style—thick steaks with the bone in the middle. Use beef, veal or lamb shanks if you have a problem getting buffalo.

Marinate the shanks.

Combine in a large pot:

4 thick-cut, osso bucco-style buffalo shanks

1/2 cup (125 ml) soy sauce

2 Tbsp. (30 ml) sesame oil

4 green onions, chopped

4 cloves garlic, minced

1 Tbsp. (15 ml) chopped fresh ginger

1 carrot, coarsely chopped

4" (10-cm) piece of daikon radish, peeled and coarsely chopped

4 dried shiitake mushrooms

2 Tbsp. (30 ml) sugar

1/2 cup (125 ml) sake or dry sherry

Marinate the meat for a couple of hours. Add:

2 cups (500 ml) water

The liquid should just cover the meat and vegetables. Bring to a boil and simmer for 1 1/2 to 2 hours, until the meat is very tender. You could serve the shanks at this point, but grilling adds a little textural interest and a smoky flavor. Remove the shanks from the braising liquid and let them cool slightly.

Make the mayonnaise.

Combine in a small bowl:

1 cup (250 ml) mayonnaise

1 Tbsp. (15 ml) sesame oil

1 green onion, white part only, finely minced

1 tsp. (5 ml) Vietnamese chili paste with garlic*

1 Tbsp. (15 ml) lemon juice

1 Tbsp. (15 ml) black sesame seeds*

Set aside.

Preheat the barbecue to medium-high or turn on the broiler and adjust the oven rack to 6" (15 cm) below the heat. Grill the shanks for 3 minutes on each side or until slightly crisp. Serve them topped with a dab of the mayonnaise and, optionally, some of the braised vegetables. A little pile of *kimchee*, the spicy cabbage pickle of Korean cuisine, would also be great.

*See The Pantry

Serving Suggestion

Combines well with Tamarind Spiced Green Beans (page 103) and Yaki Onigiri (page 141).

Mixed Wild Sushi
Platter, page 125

*Mussels with Garlic
and Chilies, page 121*

Winter

Looking West

After the snowfall

deep in the pine forest

a bough breaks.

Chinese Greens with Black Olives

This dish was inspired by one of the native dishes of Sicily. It has raisins and almonds in it, an indication of the Moorish influence on the cuisine of Sicily. Use any of the leafy Chinese greens or Italian rapini for this recipe. I am especially fond of gailan.

Make the olive mixture.

Combine in a bowl:
1/2 cup (125 ml) kalamata olives, pitted and cut in half
1/4 cup (60 ml) sun-dried tomatoes, diced
1/4 cup (60 ml) slivered, blanched almonds, toasted
1/4 cup (60 ml) raisins

Heat a sauté pan over medium heat. Add:
1/2 cup (125 ml) extra-virgin olive oil
1 clove garlic, minced

Cook the garlic for 1 minute and then add the olive mixture. Cook and stir the mixture for 2 minutes. Set aside.

Trim the woody ends off:
1 lb. (450 g) Chinese greens

Steam the greens until crisp-tender. You can tell if the greens are done by looking at the stem end. If not quite cooked there will be a white dot in the middle of the stalk. When done, the white spot will have vanished.

Divide the greens among 4 plates. Cut them in half and spoon 1/4 of the olive mixture onto each serving.

Serving Suggestion

Combines well with Calamari Ragout (page 118) and Oyster and Bacon Yaki (page 119).

Eggplant with Garlic and Goat Cheese

A bow towards California cuisine, this dish uses all of the favorite ingredients of that milieu. Use Japanese eggplants, which are sweeter and more succulent than the large globe variety. The earthiness of the garlic purée, the richness of the goat cheese and the sharp accent of the sun-dried tomatoes come together to make a truly wonderful composition.

Make the garlic purée.

Combine in a small deep pot:

10 heads of garlic, the root ends cut off to expose the cloves
vegetable oil to cover the garlic completely
1/4 cup (60 ml) extra-virgin olive oil
2 sprigs fresh thyme

Bring to a low simmer and cook for about half an hour. The garlic is done when the exposed cloves turn a very pale golden brown. Drain the hot oil into a heatproof container and reserve for salad dressings or brushing on grilled meats. When the garlic is cool enough to handle comfortably, squeeze the cloves out of the papery skins into the bowl of a food processor. Discard the skins.

Add:

2 Tbsp. (30 ml) of the reserved oil
1/4 tsp. (1.2 ml) salt
1/2 tsp. (2.5 ml) sugar

Process the garlic until smooth.

In a bowl, mix 3/4 cup (185 ml) of the garlic purée with:

1/4 cup (60 ml) creamy goat cheese

Set aside.

Preheat the barbecue to medium or turn on the broiler and adjust the oven rack to 6" (15 cm) below the heat.

Cut:

2 large Japanese eggplants

in half lengthwise. Score the cut white side with a criss-cross pattern of cuts. Brush the cut sides with a little of the garlic oil. Barbecue or broil them, cut side down, for about 5 minutes or until quite soft. Turn over and cook a further 2 minutes. Remove from the heat and cut into bite-sized chunks. Arrange each eggplant half on a plate so that it retains its original shape. Spread a generous layer of the garlic and goat cheese mixture on top and dot with:

4 sun-dried tomatoes, cut into 1/4" (.5-cm) dice

Serving Suggestion

Combines well with Pappadam Curried Oysters (page 106) and Persian Honey-Spiced Chicken (page 123).

Calamari Ragout

This is an adaptation of one of my all-time favorite dishes from one of my all-time favorite cookery writers, Richard Olney. We have made it a little more Asian, but tried not to tamper too much with the essence of the dish. For instructions on how to clean squid see the recipe for Calamari Salad with Black Beans and Ginger (page 12).

Heat a sauté pan over high heat. Add:

2 Tbsp. (30 ml) vegetable oil

Heat for 30 seconds more. Add:

2 lbs. (900 g) small squid, cleaned, cut into thick rings and patted very dry with paper towels

Stir-fry for 2 minutes. Season with:

pinch salt and pepper

Remove from the heat and set aside.

In a saucepan, heat:

2 Tbsp. (30 ml) vegetable oil

Add:

2 medium leeks, white part only, coarsely chopped
1 large shallot, minced
1 clove garlic, minced

Sweat for 10 minutes over medium-low heat with a lid on. Stir occasionally to prevent scorching and add a little water if required. Add the squid and:

1 1/2 cups (375 ml) red wine
1 tsp. (5 ml) Szechuan peppercorns, ground*
2 pieces star anise
3 strips orange zest

Cover the mixture and simmer over low heat for 40 minutes to 1 hour. The squid should be very tender.

In a small bowl combine:

2 Tbsp. (30 ml) cornstarch
3 Tbsp. (45 ml) red wine

Stir this slurry into the simmering calamari. Cook for another 2 minutes. Correct the seasoning with:

1 tsp. (5 ml) soy sauce
pinch salt and pepper

Divide among 4 bowls and serve immediately.

*See The Pantry

Serving Suggestion

Combines well with Green Onion Cakes with Lemon Dipping Sauce (page 52) and Chinese Greens with Black Olives (page 116) or with a loaf of crusty bread.

Oyster and Bacon Yaki

This is a very simple dish. It is a great favorite in the izakayas, Japanese beer halls, to which Raku owes part of its heritage. Substitute pancetta for the bacon if you want lower fat content.

Lay out:

8 large oysters
8 thin slices bacon

Wrap a piece of bacon around each oyster and thread them on bamboo skewers. Weave the skewer through the bacon and oyster so the bacon is securely attached to the oyster.

Preheat the barbecue to medium-high or turn on the broiler and adjust the oven rack to 6" (15 cm) below the heat. Grill or broil the oysters until the bacon is crisp. Turn over and crisp the other side. Serve them with:

lemon wedges

Serving Suggestion

Combines well with Chinese Greens with Black Olives (page 116) and Spicy Shrimp Onigiri (page 142).

Jumbo Prawns with Creole Butter

Prawns go very well with any kind of compound butter. The butter accentuates the richness of the prawns. I remember sitting in our tiny, four-mat room in Tokyo preparing a variation on these prawns after a trip to the famous Tsukiji fish market. Heaven! We use the largest prawns available because they tend to shrink somewhat on the grill.

Make the creole butter.

Combine in the bowl of a food processor or blender.

1/2 cup (125 ml) butter, softened
1 tsp. (5 ml) fresh thyme leaves
2 cloves garlic, minced
2 Tbsp. (30 ml) coarsely ground black pepper
1/4 tsp. (1.2 ml) cayenne pepper
2 Tbsp. (30 ml) lemon juice

Process until combined and set aside.

Peel and devein:
12 jumbo prawns

Thread them, three to a skewer, on bamboo skewers.

Heat the barbecue to hot or turn on the broiler and adjust oven rack to 6" (15 cm) below the heat. Grill the prawns for 2 minutes on each side or until they are done to your liking.

Spoon some of the creole butter onto 4 warm serving plates and arrange the prawns on top.

Serving Suggestion

Combines well with Tamarind Spiced Green Beans (page 103) and Yaki Onigiri (page 141).

Mussels with Garlic and Chilies

This mussel dish features prodigious amounts of garlic added at various stages and in different forms. The basis for the sauce is Japanese dashi soup stock. It has a smoky richness that complements the flavors of the Mexican chilies that we use here. The konbu kelp and dried bonito flakes are available at Japanese markets. You can substitute clam nectar or instant dashi soup stock powder, which are available in many supermarkets, for the dashi. You can make this dish in a soup pot, or if you have four small hotpots, serving one per person makes a nice presentation. Adjust the measurements accordingly.

Make the dashi soup stock.

In a saucepan, place:
2" (5-cm) piece of konbu kelp
4 cups (1 l) water

Bring to a boil, turn off the heat and add:
1/2 cup (125 ml) dried bonito flakes

Let the soup stand for 15 minutes, then strain the stock into a bowl and discard the solids.

Make the chili paste.

Roast:
4 ancho chilies*
over the burner on your stove or in a sauté pan. It won't take long (about a minute per side). The chilies will puff up when done. Be careful they do not burn. Snip the stem end off the chilies and discard the seeds. Put the chilies in a bowl, cover with boiling water and let them soften for 20 minutes. Put the chilies into the bowl of a food processor with:
3 cloves garlic, or 2 Tbsp. (30 ml) roasted garlic purée (see page 117)
1/2 tsp. (2.5 ml) dried thyme
1/2 tsp. (2.5 ml) dried oregano
1/4 cup (60 ml) olive oil
salt and pepper to taste

Process until smooth.

Prepare the mussels.

Wash and debeard:
60 mussels

Bring 3/4 cup (185 ml) of the dashi soup stock to a boil in a large Japanese hotpot. Add the mussels and:
1/2 cup (125 ml) chili paste
4 cloves garlic, minced
1 Tbsp. (15 ml) Thai fish sauce*

Cover the hotpot, bring to a boil and simmer for 1 minute. Add:
1 Tbsp. (15 ml) Thai fried garlic*
1/4 cup (60 ml) chopped cilantro leaves

Cover again and cook a further 30 seconds.

When you are finished eating the mussels, the broth from this dish is fantastic with a cup of cooked rice stirred into it.

*See The Pantry

Serving Suggestion

Combines well with Chinese Greens with Black Olives (page 116) and Yaki Onigiri (page 141).

Red Snapper with Garlic Ancho Chili Spread

We came up with this recipe for a wine- and food-tasting dinner. This particular dinner was a celebration of allium, and each course featured garlic in heavy doses. This dish is a little time-consuming as it calls for roasted garlic purée, but if you make a big batch of the purée it will last for a couple of weeks in the fridge and can be used in a variety of dishes and as a spread for bread. Make sure your whole family eats it at the same time!

Serving Suggestion

Combines well with Sweet Potato with Soy Butter (page 101) and Yaki Onigiri (page 141).

Make the garlic purée (see page 117).

Make the chili paste.

Combine in a bowl:

1/2 cup (125 ml) Mexican-style chili powder

1 Tbsp. (15 ml) ground cumin

1 Tbsp. (15 ml) ground coriander

1 clove garlic, grated

1/4 tsp. (1.2 ml) ground cloves

1/4 tsp. (1.2 ml) ground allspice

1/2 tsp. (2.5 ml) ground anise seed

1/4 cup (60 ml) olive oil

Set aside. This will keep in the refrigerator for weeks.

Make the tomatillo vinaigrette.

Combine in the bowl of a food processor or blender:

9 medium tomatillos (see page 69), grilled or broiled until soft and brown on the outside

1 clove garlic

1 small bunch cilantro

1/4 tsp. (1.2 ml) salt

2 Tbsp. (30 ml) rice wine vinegar*

1/4 cup (60 ml) olive oil

Process until almost smooth, but still a little chunky. Combine 1/2 cup (125 ml) of the garlic purée and 1/4 cup (60 ml) of the chili paste in a small bowl.

Have ready:

4 6-oz. (180-g) filets of red snapper

Preheat the barbecue to medium-high or turn on the broiler and adjust the oven rack to 6" (15 cm) below the heat. Grill or broil the fish for 2-3 minutes on one side. Remove from the heat and spread the cooked side with the chili paste/garlic purée. Grill the uncooked side for 2-3 minutes, or until the fish is done to your liking.

If you are using the oven, don't put the paste on until the fish is almost completely cooked on both sides, then spread it on the top surface and let it cook for about 30 seconds. Be careful as it burns easily.

Remove to 4 plates. Garnish with the tomatillo vinaigrette and a sprig of cilantro or a husk from the tomatillos.

*See The Pantry

Persian Honey-Spiced Chicken

The flavors in this dish are simple but combine to produce something that is wholly satisfying. The interesting part of this dish is the spice and nut mix that is sprinkled on the chicken. It is called a dukkah, *and there are many different versions. A little familiar and a little exotic, this dish is a winner.*

Make the marinade.

Combine in a flat bowl:
1/4 cup (60 ml) lemon juice
1/2 cup (125 ml) olive oil
1/2 tsp. (2.5 ml) salt
1/4 tsp. (1.2 ml) pepper
1 tsp. (5 ml) dried oregano
1 clove garlic, minced

Cut into 1" (2.5-cm) cubes:
4 skinless boneless chicken breasts or 6 boneless thighs

Thread the chicken onto 8 bamboo skewers. Place the chicken skewers in a flat pan with the marinade. Marinate for half an hour.

Make the spice mix, or *dukkah.*

Combine in a mortar:
2 Tbsp. (30 ml) toasted sesame seeds
1 Tbsp. (15 ml) toasted coriander seeds
3 Tbsp. (45 ml) hazelnuts, toasted and skinned
1/4 tsp. (1.2 ml) salt

Grind them with a pestle until a crumbly, cornmeal-like texture is achieved.

Preheat the barbecue to medium-high or turn on the broiler and adjust the oven rack to 6" (15 cm) below the heat. Barbecue or broil the skewers for 3-5 minutes on each side, or until thoroughly cooked. Arrange on 4 plates. Drizzle with a small amount of:
honey

Sprinkle with the dukkah.

Serving Suggestion

Combines well with Pappadam Curried Oysters (page 106) and Eggplant with Garlic and Goat Cheese (page 117).

Wild Sushi

The idea for wild sushi was created in response to people walking into Raku, mistaking it for a Japanese restaurant and asking "Where is the sushi?"

The reason Laurie and I hadn't included sushi on the original menu was two-fold: we thought the sushi market was well served, and we were both a little tired of it. We had just spent a whole year making and eating sushi five days a week, at a sushi school in Tokyo. We would arrive early in the morning to make the rice for the day. A couple of hours later all the other students and the fresh fish arrived. The rest of the morning was devoted to learning how to clean, cut and prepare the different varieties of fish and seafood. We then made ourselves lunch—sushi, of course. By the end of the year Laurie was so sick of sushi, she could only eat miso soup.

In the afternoon we practiced making rice balls. We would each cut 30 or 40 little pieces of a small, strongly flavored fish called kohada. We then made 30 pieces of sushi with the rice balls and the fish, and when we were done we would strip the pieces of fish from the rice, throw the rice back into the bucket, line up our pieces of fish and do it all over again! This went on all afternoon in the heat of the Japanese summer. When we could not stand looking at or smelling the kohada any more, we would take little rectangular pieces of newspaper that represented nori

When the old pond

gets a new frog

it's a new pond

–Author unknown

seaweed (nori being much too expensive to waste on practice), cut the (by this time stinking) kohada into strips, and make them into the various rolls. We learned a lot at the sushi school, but when we returned to Vancouver making sushi was not a top priority.

Five years later we were able to approach the subject of sushi again and applied our usual method of mixing and matching cuisines to come up with some unusual sushi rolls.

All the ingredients you need to prepare sushi can be found in Japanese markets. If you can't find one, ask your local sushi bar where they get their supplies and they will point you in the right direction.

Sushi Rice

Hundreds of years ago, the Japanese discovered that there is an enzyme in cooked rice that acts as a preservative. When they were going on a long journey they would surround a piece of fish with rice and wrap it tightly in cloth. Several days into their trip they would take the fish out of the rice, discard the rice and eat the fish. Someone eventually decided to try the rice and found it to be pleasingly sour. This evolved into the sweet and sour rice that we know as sushi rice today.

Sushi rice is the only required element when making sushi. The toppings are optional and limited only by your imagination.

In your quest for the zen of sushi-making, keep two things in mind. When a true sushi master mixes the vinegar into the rice, the grains of rice should all be aligned in the same direction. The same should be true when forming the rice ball for a piece of sushi!

Wash thoroughly in a strainer:

5 cups (1250 ml) Japanese-style short-grained rice

Put it into a rice cooker or heavy pot.

Add:

6 1/4 cups (1560 ml) water
1 3" (7.5-cm) square of konbu kelp
1/4 cup (60 ml) sake

Cook according to the directions that came with the rice cooker. If you are using a pot, cover and bring to a boil. Boil over high heat for 2 minutes. Reduce the heat to medium and boil for a further 5 minutes. Reduce the heat to low and cook for 15 minutes more. Turn off the heat and let the pot stand, still tightly covered, for 10 more minutes. Remove the kelp and discard.

While the rice is cooking, prepare the sushi vinegar.

Combine in a bowl:

4 cups (1 l) rice wine vinegar*
1 2/3 cups (410 ml) sugar
1/3 cup (80 ml) salt
1 Tbsp. (15 ml) apple cider vinegar
1 Tbsp. (15 ml) mirin*

Stir until the sugar and salt are dissolved. This recipe makes twice as much sushi vinegar as you need for this amount of rice, but it keeps indefinitely in a jar stored at room temperature.

Empty the rice into a wide, shallow bowl or tub and add 2 cups (500 ml) of the sushi vinegar.

Using a rice paddle or a large spoon, break up and combine the rice and vinegar with horizontal cutting strokes. This cutting motion tosses the mixture without crushing the grains of rice. When the rice and vinegar are well combined, cover with a damp, lint-free kitchen towel and set aside for 15 minutes.

The rice can be made ahead and kept at room temperature, covered with the damp cloth and a lid, for several hours. It should not be refrigerated or left overnight.

This amount of rice will make about 10 rolls, enough for 4 or 5 people. If you only want to make a little sushi, reduce the amounts of rice and vinegar proportionately.

Repeat the cutting and tossing routine once more and let sit covered with the cloth for another 10 minutes. The sushi rice is now ready to use.

If you want to add some theatrics to the preparation, instead of covering the rice and letting it sit, have a friend fan the rice as you toss it. Even better, try to do both things yourself!

Rolling Sushi

All the recipes that follow are for rolls. There are several other types of sushi, but rolls (maki) are the favorites with most of our customers. There are two basic rolls: regular nori sushi rolls and inside-out rolls. Regular sushi rolls have the seaweed (nori) on the outside, wrapped around rice and a filling.

It is helpful to have a bamboo sushi rolling mat. These are available in Japanese markets and many cookware shops.

Regular Sushi Rolls

On top of a bamboo sushi rolling mat place:

1 whole sheet of nori seaweed, shiny side down

Spread:

1 cup (250 ml) prepared sushi rice

in a 1/4" (.5-cm) layer on the nori, leaving a 1" (2.5-cm) strip of the seaweed uncovered by rice at the top of the sheet.

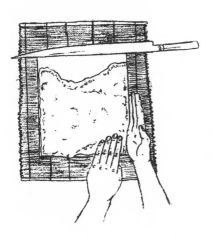

Before handling the rice, dip your hands in a bowl of water, then shake off the excess water. Whenever your hands start to feel sticky, wet them again.

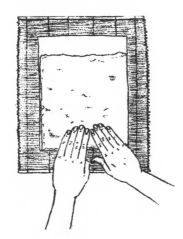

Lay the filling, or core, ingredients in strips across the rice. Keep the ingredients grouped together to make rolling easier.

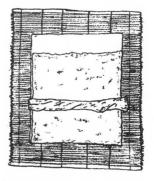

To roll, hold the bottom edge of the mat with your thumbs and the core ingredients with your fingers.

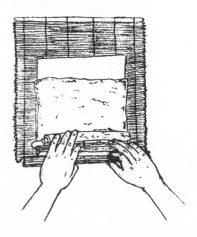

Roll the bottom edge of the mat up and over the core ingredients, so that the bottom edge of the nori is touching the rice on the other side of the ingredients.

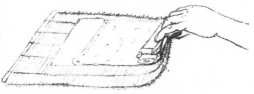

Press the mat to tighten the roll, then lift the bottom edge of the mat out of the way and complete the roll, ending with the seam on the bottom.

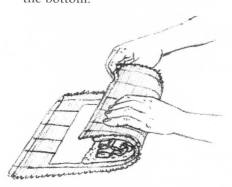

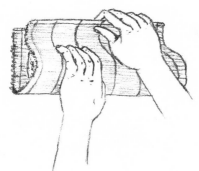

Press the mat around the roll to shape it and then place the roll to the side with the seam down.

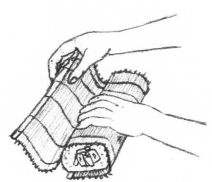

Cut the roll into 8-12 pieces with a sharp knife, making long, clean strokes. Wipe the blade of your knife with a wet cloth between each cut.

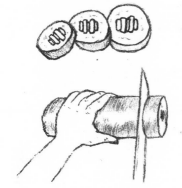

Arrange on a plate and serve with the appropriate dipping sauce.

Inside-Out Sushi Rolls

These rolls have the rice on the outside and the seaweed and filling on the inside. The trick to inside-out rolls is to waterproof your rolling mat. You do this by sliding the mat into a large-sized freezer bag. Besides being waterproof, it makes cleaning the mat easy. If you don't have a freezer bag, wrap your mat in a large sheet of plastic wrap.

Cut:

1 sheet of nori

into 2 equal pieces. Place 1 of the pieces on the prepared rolling mat, shiny side down.

Cover the nori completely with:

3/4 cup (185 ml) prepared sushi rice

The rice should be spread evenly to a depth of about 1/3" (.75 cm).

Flip the sheet over so that the rice-covered side is down. (Don't worry, the rice is sticky and will not fall off.) Align the bottom edge of the sheet about 1/3" (.75 cm) from the bottom of the mat.

Put the core ingredients onto the nori and roll in the same manner as the regular roll. Don't use too many core ingredients; if you do the rolls will not seal properly.

Tuna and Sea Asparagus Roll

Sea asparagus is a tidal plant that is harvested from the wild along the north coast of British Columbia. It has a great crunchy texture and a salty taste that complements the soft rich flavors and textures of the tuna. Sea asparagus is quite difficult to come by. You can find it—or, rather, request it—at some fishmongers or you can substitute strips of cucumber or spears of asparagus. The taste will be different but also very good.

Make the basil dipping sauce.

In a blender or food processor combine:

1 cup (250 ml) packed basil leaves
1/4 cup (60 ml) lemon juice
1 tsp. (5 ml) Dijon mustard
1/2 cup (125 ml) extra-virgin olive oil
1 Tbsp. (15 ml) vegetable oil
1/2 tsp. (2.5 ml) sugar
salt and pepper to taste

Process to a thick purée.

For each roll, lay out:

1 oz. (30 g) raw albacore tuna cut into a 1/2" x 1/2" x 8" (1 cm x 1 cm x 20 cm) strip*
1/4 cup (60 ml) sea asparagus
2 strips roasted red bell pepper (see page 137)

To assemble the roll, follow the regular sushi roll method up until the point where the core ingredients are added. Spread a small spoonful of the basil sauce in a line across the middle of the rice. Lay out the rest of the ingredients on top of the basil sauce and roll according to the regular method.

Cut and serve with a little more of the basil sauce as a dip.

*See The Pantry

Cajun Crab and Avocado Roll

The California roll is by far the favorite with sushi patrons all over North America. We have adapted it by moving it to a different state. The characteristic fiery flavors of Cajun cooking are provided in this roll by the Louisiana mayonnaise. You do not have to blacken anything in this recipe, I promise! (Whoops— forgot about the peppers!)

Make the Louisiana mayonnaise.

Combine:

1 cup (250 ml) mayonnaise

3 Tbsp. (45 ml) Louisiana hot sauce

1/2 tsp. (2.5 ml) dried thyme

1/4 tsp. (1.2 ml) ground cumin

1/4 tsp. (1.2 ml) ground coriander

1 Tbsp. (15 ml) lemon juice

salt and pepper to taste

For each roll, lay out:

4 Tbsp. (60 ml) lump crabmeat

3 slices avocado

1 8″ (20-cm) piece of green onion top

4 strips roasted red bell pepper (see page 137)

To assemble the roll, follow the regular sushi roll method up until the point where the core ingredients are added. Spread a small spoonful of mayonnaise in a line across the rice. Lay out the rest of the ingredients on top of the mayonnaise and roll according to the regular method.

Cut and serve with the Louisiana mayonnaise as a dip.

Crisp Shrimp Fried Rice Roll

In our wildest dreams we could not have imagined how popular this roll would be. It was born out of dissatisfaction with the traditional tempura shrimp roll, which promised a crunch that was never forthcoming. We decided that the rice had to be crunchy, so I suggested barbecuing the roll. This was all right but our sous-chef at the time, Sisley Killam, suggested deep-frying the roll to get the crunch. We tried it and a classic was born.

Make the soy lime dipping sauce.

Combine in a bowl:

1 cup (250 ml) soy sauce
1/2 cup (125 ml) sugar
1/4 cup (60 ml) lime juice
zest of 2 limes
1" (2.5-cm) piece fresh ginger, grated
2 cloves garlic, minced

Mix until the sugar is dissolved.

Prepare the prawns.

Allowing 3 prawns per roll, skewer as many:

black tiger prawns, shell on, headless

as you need. Skewer them from the head end to the tail end so that the prawn is straight on the skewer. This will keep the prawns from curling up when they are cooked.

Bring a pot of salted water to a boil. Add the prepared prawns, turn off the heat and cook the prawns for 1 minute. Drain and cover the prawns with cold water to stop the cooking process. Remove the prawns from the skewers and shell them.

For each roll, lay out:

3 prawns
1 piece green onion top
2 strips roasted red bell pepper (see page 137)

To roll the sushi, follow the method for rolling inside-out rolls.

When the rolls are made, heat 1/2" (1 cm) of:

vegetable oil

in an 8" (20-cm) skillet to 350°F (175°C). Use a deep-fry thermometer to check the oil temperature. When the oil is hot, add the sushi roll. Stand back, as it will hiss and spit. Cook 2-3 minutes on each side until uniformly brown all over.

Cut into 8 pieces and serve with the soy lime dipping sauce.

Gado Gado Sushi Roll

People usually associate fish with sushi rolls. We like to challenge these preconceptions and one of the most successful challenges has been vegetarian rolls. Gado gado is a popular arranged vegetable salad from Indonesia.

Prepare the peanut dipping sauce.

Combine in a bowl:

1/2 cup (125 ml) smooth peanut butter
1/4 cup (60 ml) apple cider vinegar
1/4 cup (60 ml) soy sauce
2 Tbsp. (30 ml) grated fresh ginger
1 clove garlic, grated
2 Tbsp. (30 ml) lime juice
1/4 tsp. (1.2 ml) Vietnamese chili sauce with garlic*
1 Tbsp. (15 ml) sugar
1 Tbsp. (15 ml) sesame oil

Mix thoroughly. Thin to a saucelike consistency with water.

For each roll, lay out:

2 pieces dried flavored tofu, 1/4" x 1/4" x 4" (.6 cm x .6 cm x 10 cm)*
6 green beans, trimmed and blanched
1 8" (20-cm) piece of green onion top
2 strips roasted red bell pepper (see page 137)
piece of cucumber, 1/4" x 1/4" x 8" (.6 cm x .6 cm x 20 cm)

To assemble the roll, follow the regular sushi roll method.

Cut and serve with a little of the peanut dipping sauce.

*See The Pantry

Grilled Vegetable Roll

This roll is a variation of one of my favorite summer salads. It never fails to transport me to the hills of Italy. The earthy flavors of the roasted vegetables combine beautifully with the basil sauce and nori. This recipe makes enough salad and dip for about 10 rolls. Use any leftover salad as an accompaniment to grilled meat.

Prepare the basil sauce.

In a blender or food processor combine:

1 cup (250 ml) packed basil leaves
1/4 cup (60 ml) lemon juice
1 tsp. (5 ml) Dijon mustard
1/2 cup (125 ml) extra-virgin olive oil
1 Tbsp. (15 ml) vegetable oil
1/2 tsp. (2.5 ml) sugar
salt and pepper to taste

Process to a thick purée.

Prepare the grilled vegetables. Preheat the barbecue to high or turn on the broiler and adjust the oven rack to 6" (15 cm) below the heat.

Brush:
olive oil
on the cut sides of:
1 8" (20-cm) zucchini, sliced lengthwise into 1/4" (.5-cm) pieces
1 Japanese eggplant, sliced lengthwise into 1/4" (.5-cm) pieces
1 small red onion, cut across the grain into 1/4" (.5-cm) slices and secured with toothpicks

Grill or broil for 2 or 3 minutes on each side. Cool and cut lengthwise into 1/4" (.5-cm) strips.

Roast the bell pepper.

Rub:
olive oil
on:
1 large red bell pepper

Grill or broil until the skin is black. Turn the pepper to the next side and repeat until the whole pepper is black. Place in a plastic bag to steam for 10 minutes. Remove the pepper from the bag and peel the skin off. It should come off very easily. Remove the core and lay the flesh out flat. Cut the pepper into 1/4" (.5-cm) strips.

Put all the grilled vegetables into a bowl.

Mix in:
10 pitted Kalamata olives, torn in half
2 Tbsp. (30 ml) capers
2 Tbsp. (30 ml) fresh oregano leaves
2 Tbsp. (30 ml) balsamic vinegar
4 Tbsp. (60 ml) extra-virgin olive oil
salt and pepper to taste

To assemble the roll, follow the regular sushi roll method.

Cut and serve with a little of the basil dipping sauce.

Korean Salmon Roll

This roll is the latest in a line of derivations from the Korean raw beef dish called yukke. *The pink salmon and the black and white sesame seeds on the outside of the roll make a beautiful presentation.*

Make the Korean dipping sauce.

Combine in a bowl:

1 cup (250 ml) soy sauce
1/2 cup (125 ml) sugar
1" (2.5-cm) piece grated fresh ginger
3 cloves garlic, minced
1 tsp. (5 ml) Vietnamese chili paste with garlic*
1 Tbsp. (15 ml) sesame oil

Stir until the sugar is dissolved and the other ingredients are thoroughly mixed.

For each roll, lay out:

1 strip raw salmon, about 1/4" x 1/4" x 8" (.6 cm x .6 cm x 20 cm)*
1 piece green onion top
2 strips roasted red bell pepper (see page 137)

To make the roll, follow the method for making inside-out rolls.

To finish the rolls, mix:

1/4 cup (60 ml) toasted white sesame seeds
1/4 cup (60 ml) black sesame seeds
in a flat dish as long as the rolls.

Roll the sushi roll in the sesame seed mixture.

Cut the roll into 8 or 10 pieces and serve with the Korean dipping sauce.

*See The Pantry

Paella Sushi Roll

This roll was inspired by the famous Spanish rice dish, paella. The saffron mayonnaise in this roll marries with other ingredients to give a surreal impression of Spain gone Japanese.

Make the saffron mayonnaise.

Bring to a boil:

2 Tbsp. (30 ml) dry white wine

Add:

1/4 tsp. (1.2 ml) saffron

Remove from the heat and cool to room temperature.

Combine the saffron steeped in wine with:

1 cup (250 ml) mayonnaise
1 Tbsp. (15 ml) lemon juice
salt and pepper to taste

For each roll, lay out:

4 pieces of ham or smoked duck, 4" x 1/4" x 1/4" (10 cm x .6 cm x .6 cm) in size
3 Tbsp. (45 ml) fresh lump crabmeat
1 8" (20-cm) piece green onion top
4 strips roasted red bell pepper (see page 137)

To assemble the roll, follow the regular sushi roll method up to the point where the core ingredients are added. Spread a small spoonful of mayonnaise in a line across the rice. Lay out the rest of the ingredients on top of the mayonnaise and roll according to the regular method.

Cut and serve with a little more of the saffron mayonnaise as a dip.

Chicken Satay Sushi Roll

I know that chicken in a sushi roll sounds strange, but this roll has a great rationale. In Indonesia, the traditional accompaniments for satay, barbecued meat skewers, are pressed rice cakes and pickled cucumber. We have combined all of these in a roll and serve it with a peanut dipping sauce.

Make the peanut dipping sauce.

Combine in a bowl:

1/2 cup (125 ml) smooth peanut butter

1/4 cup (60 ml) apple cider vinegar

1/4 cup (60 ml) soy sauce

2 Tbsp. (30 ml) grated fresh ginger

1 clove garlic, grated

2 Tbsp. (30 ml) lime juice

1/4 tsp. (1.2 ml) Vietnamese chili sauce with garlic*

1 Tbsp. (15 ml) sugar

1 Tbsp. (15 ml) sesame oil

Mix thoroughly. Thin to a saucelike consistency with water.

Prepare the chicken.

Cut:

1 skinless, boneless chicken breast

into strips that are 1/2" x 1/2" x 6" (1 cm x 1 cm x 15 cm). Thread on bamboo skewers.

Combine in a bowl:

1 clove garlic, minced

2 Tbsp. (30 ml) tamarind concentrate*

1 Tbsp. (15 ml) sugar

2 Tbsp. (30 ml) soy sauce

Add the chicken and marinate for 20 minutes.

Preheat the barbecue to high or turn on the broiler and adjust the oven rack to 6" (15 cm) beneath the heat. Grill or broil the chicken strips until done, about 3 minutes per side. Cool and remove from the skewers.

For each roll, lay out:

2-3 chicken strips

1 8" (20-cm) piece green onion top

2 strips roasted red bell pepper (see page 137)

1 piece cucumber, 1/4" x 1/4" x 8" (.6 cm x .6 cm x 20 cm)

To assemble the roll, follow the regular sushi roll method.

Cut and serve with a little of the peanut dipping sauce.

*See The Pantry

Yaki Onigiri

Onigiri *are the true sandwiches of Japan. They can be found in every child's lunch kit and are a feature of thousands of take-out shops. They are nothing more than rice balls formed into a triangular shape. The most common variety are filled with a little plum paste or salted salmon and wrapped with a piece of nori seaweed. Grilled rice balls,* yaki onigiri, *are very typical* izakaya, *or bar, food.*

Make the tare yaki sauce (see page 17).

Wash thoroughly in a strainer:
3 cups (750 ml) Japanese-style short-grained rice

Put it into a rice cooker or heavy pot with:
3 3/4 cups (935 ml) water

Cook according to the directions that came with the rice cooker. If you are using a pot, cover and bring to a boil. Boil over high heat for 2 minutes. Reduce the heat to medium and boil for a further 5 minutes. Reduce the heat to low and cook for 15 minutes more. Turn off the heat and let the pot stand, still tightly covered, for 10 more minutes.

Empty the rice into a bowl and break it up slightly. Let it cool for 5 minutes. Wet your hands and pick up a handful of rice, about 1/2 cup (125 ml). Form it into a triangular shape. Press quite firmly, as the rice must not fall apart when you put it on the barbecue. When each rice ball is formed put it on a plate and repeat the procedure until all the rice is formed into balls. You should get 10 to 12 rice balls.

Preheat the barbecue to medium-high or turn on the broiler and adjust the oven rack to 6" (15 cm) below the heat. Dab a little oil on either side of the rice ball and grill or broil until crisp and brown on each side.

Dip the onigiri into the tare yaki sauce and serve 2 per person.

Spicy Shrimp Onigiri

This is one of our very popular variations on the onigiri theme. It features an adaptation of an Indian spicy shrimp pickle from Charmain Solomon's Asian Cookbook. *All the spices and pastes can be found in Indian groceries, health food shops and bulk food stores. If you can't get one or two of the spices, just leave them out.*

Make the spicy shrimp pickle.

Combine in the bowl of a food processor:

6 cloves garlic
1 1" (2.5-cm) piece fresh ginger

Process until finely chopped. Add:

1/2 cup (125 ml) rice vinegar

Purée.

Place in a large saucepan:

1 Tbsp. (15 ml) ground cumin
3 Tbsp. (45 ml) turmeric
1 Tbsp. (15 ml) chili powder
1 Tbsp. (15 ml) paprika
1 Tbsp. (15 ml) ground coriander
2 curry leaves, crumbled
**1 Tbsp. (15 ml) red mustard
    seed***
**1 Tbsp. (15 ml) yellow mustard
    seed***
1 tsp. (5 ml) powdered ginger
1 tsp. (5 ml) ground allspice
1 tsp. (5 ml) anise seed
1 tsp. (5 ml) fennel seed
1 tsp. (5 ml) ground cardamom
3/4 cup (185 ml) vegetable oil

Cook the spices in the oil for 1 minute over medium heat. Add the vinegar mixture and cook over low heat for 5 minutes.

Add:

**2 lbs. (900 g) machine-peeled,
    cooked baby shrimp**
1 Tbsp. (15 ml) Thai fish sauce*
**1 tsp. (5 ml) Kashmiri masala
    paste (see page 113)**

Cook over low heat, stirring frequently until the oil starts to separate from the mixture, about 20 minutes. This pickle will keep covered in the fridge for a couple of weeks.

Wash thoroughly in a strainer:

**3 cups (750 ml) Japanese-style
    short-grained rice**

Put it into a rice cooker or heavy pot with:

3 3/4 cups (935 ml) water

Cook according to the directions that came with the rice cooker. If you are using a pot, cover and bring to a boil. Boil over high heat for 2 minutes. Reduce the heat to medium and boil for a further 5 minutes. Reduce the heat to low and cook for 15 minutes more. Turn off the heat and let the pot stand, still tightly covered, for 10 more minutes.

Empty the rice out into a bowl and break it up slightly. Let it cool for 5 minutes. Wet your hands and pick up a handful of rice, about 1/2 cup (125 ml). Form it into a triangular shape. Press quite firmly, as the rice must not fall apart when you put it on the barbecue. When each rice ball is formed put it on a plate and repeat the procedure until all of the rice is formed into balls. You should get 10 to 12 rice balls.

Preheat your barbecue to medium-high or turn on the broiler and adjust the oven rack to 6" (15 cm) below the heat. Dab a little oil on either side of the rice ball. Grill or broil until crisp and brown on each side.

Put two rice balls on each plate and top each with a large spoonful of the shrimp pickle.

*See The Pantry

Desserts

esserts are a passion for most people, one way or the other. For some, the whole preceding meal has been nothing but a pretext to get to the dessert. For others, dessert represents everything that is bad about our diet. I think that to be a baker or dessert chef you must be a member of the first group. I fall somewhere in the middle on desserts—they are not a passion for me. I think desserts require a different set of skills and a different muse. For that reason I like to keep the desserts at Raku very simple but still interesting and satisfying. I have included the three most popular desserts that we serve, as some of our regulars would never have forgiven me if I hadn't.

Seasonal Crème Brulée

Our crème brulées are the most popular dessert we serve. We have customers who travel the world, including a few who live part of the year in Paris, who come back time and again saying they are the best they have ever tasted. The concept is simple: keep the custard creamy, add seasonal fruit and, where appropriate, a sprinkle of grated chocolate. To finish the brulées you need one special piece of equipment—a blowtorch!

Prepare the custard.

Combine in a mixing bowl:
4 egg yolks
1 3/4 cups (435 ml) whipping cream
1/4 cup (60 ml) sugar

Stir until the sugar is dissolved.

Preheat the oven to 325°F (165°C).

Assemble 4 1/2-cup (125-ml) ramekins.

Into each ramekin place:
5 fresh raspberries
1 tsp. (5 ml) grated semisweet chocolate

Pour in enough custard to fill each ramekin. Place the ramekins in a baking pan filled with 1/2" (1 cm) boiling water. Place the pan in the oven and cook for 30-35 minutes, or until the custard is set.

The brulées can be made to this point days in advance and kept covered in the refrigerator.

To finish the brulées, sprinkle each custard with:
1 Tbsp. (15 ml) sugar

Using a blowtorch, caramelize the sugar on top of each custard by playing the flame of the torch over the sugar until it has melted and turned brown.

Serve immediately.

Variations: In July use raspberries. August calls for blackberries. In September we use blueberries. In October and November cranberries, cooked until soft with a little orange juice and sugar, are wonderful. In December and January we use candied ginger chunks instead of fruit. In February, March and April, try dried apricots or peaches simmered in a little wine or fruit juice. In May and June use fresh strawberries tossed with a little orange liqueur.

Coconut Crème Caramel

This crème caramel was probably the first dessert we put on the menu. It is simple and a fine example of fusion cooking, substituting coconut milk for part of the cream.

Make the caramel.

Set out:
4 1/2-cup (125-ml) ramekins

Put:
1/2 cup (125 ml) water
into the bottom of a saucepan.

Add:
1 cup (250 ml) sugar
in a pile in the center of the pan. Be careful the sugar does not splash up onto the sides of the pan as any grain of unmelted sugar can cause the caramel to crystallize. Cook over high heat. The mixture will dissolve, then start to bubble furiously. Watch it carefully for signs of browning and when it starts to turn golden brown, remove it from the heat and give the pan a gentle swirl to distribute the color. The heat of the pan will continue to brown the sugar, so be careful you don't burn it. Carefully pour the caramel into the ramekins, coating the bottom of each one.

(For easy clean-up fill the pan with hot water and return it to a boil. You will find that the boiling water dissolves all the remaining caramel, making clean-up a breeze.)

Preheat the oven to 350° F (175°C).

Make the custard.

Combine:
1 2/3 cups (410 ml) coconut milk
1/3 cup (80 ml) whipping cream
1/3 cup (80 ml) sugar
3 egg yolks
2 whole eggs

Whisk until smooth and the sugar is dissolved.

Pour the custard into each of the ramekins. Put the ramekins into a baking pan filled with 1/2" (1 cm) of boiling water. Bake in the oven for 1/2 hour, or until the center looks firm. Remove and cool.

When the custards are cool, run a thin-bladed knife around the edge of each one to loosen it, then turn them out onto small individual dessert plates.

Grapefruit Sorbet

This dessert could also be called a fruit ice or granita. It is very refreshing and can be used in the middle of a multi-course meal as well as at the end.

Combine in a saucepan:

**4 cups (1 l) freshly squeezed
grapefruit juice**
1 cup (250 ml) sugar

Stir over medium heat until the sugar is dissolved.

Pour into a flat, shallow container to cool. Freeze, covered, overnight. The next day use a large spoon to scrape the ice into small shards. Transfer the sorbet to a plastic container and keep frozen until ready to use.

Serve in small dessert bowls.

Index

About the author

Photo: Robert Karpa

Trevor Hooper is chef and owner of Vancouver's highly successful Raku restaurant. He has trained at Leith's School of Food and Wine in London, England, and Sushi Daigaku, a world renowned cooking school in Tokyo, Japan.

Trevor and his partner Laurie Robertson opened Raku to immediate critical and popular acclaim in 1990. It was voted restaurant of the year by *Vancouver Magazine* in 1992 and chosen as a top Vancouver restaurant by *Gourmet Magazine* in 1993 and 1996. Raku continues to pioneer the exciting style of cooking known as Pacific Rim fusion.

Trevor now divides his time between managing the restaurant, teaching, writing, and his family.

Notes